Integrating Information Literacy into the Higher Education Curriculum

Ilene F. Rockman and Associates

Integrating Information Literacy into the Higher Education Curriculum

Practical Models for Transformation

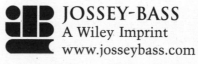

JOSSEY-BASS
A Wiley Imprint
www.josseybass.com

Published by Jossey-Bass
A Wiley Imprint
989 Market Street, San Francisco, CA 94103-1741   www.josseybass.com

Jossey-Bass books and products are available through most bookstores. To contact Jossey-Bass directly call our Customer Care Department within the U.S. at 800-956-7739, outside the U.S. at 317-572-3986 or fax 317-572-4002.

Jossey-Bass also publishes its books in a variety of electronic formats. Some content that appears in print may not be available in electronic books.

Library of Congress Cataloging-in-Publication Data

Integrating information literacy into the higher education curriculum: Practical models for transformation / Ilene Rockman and associates.— 1st ed.
    p. cm. — (The Jossey-Bass higher and adult education series)
  Includes bibliographical references and index.
    ISBN 0-7879-6527-8 (alk. paper)
  1. Information literacy—Study and teaching (Higher)—United States.   2. Education, Higher—Curricula—United States.   3.   Academic libraries—Relations with faculty and curriculum—United States.   I. Rockman, Ilene F.   II. Series.
    ZA3075.I57 2004
    028.7'071'173—dc22   2003027930

Printed in the United States of America
FIRST EDITION
HB Printing   10 9 8 7 6 5 4 3 2 1

To Fred, for his love, encouragement, and never-ending support
To John, Charlotte, and Joe for their superb information
literacy skills which allowed me to complete this project
and
To Leon and Margaret, for always being there

Contents

Foreword

It really is a miracle! For all practical purposes, information literacy only appeared on the radar screens of educators and librarians with the release of the American Library Association Presidential Committee on Information Literacy Final Report in Washington, D.C., in January 1989. Now, fifteen years later, information literacy is widely addressed in K–12 and higher education settings in the United States and abroad; national standards of student learning outcomes have been established at the K–12 and undergraduate levels; and the topic is increasingly being addressed in forums outside of the library profession.

What is even more miraculous is that, perhaps for the first time, librarians are finding themselves thrust into leadership roles in the learning process. This, of course, has created its own set of challenges, especially since the kind of leadership needed is not one based on control but rather one of servant leadership. In this role, librarians encourage, support, and nudge faculty in the establishment of learning priorities which ensure that students develop the abilities that will allow them to be effective lifelong learners. For many, fulfilling this is much harder than designing a program and then trying to sell it to faculty and administrators.

The authors in this book are good representatives of those in higher education who are not only committed to information literacy but who relish moving into leadership roles. Because of them and other pioneers like them, information literacy efforts on many campuses have now matured and can provide both models for success and indicators of quality. While the current well-founded efforts of the Association of College and Research Libraries (ACRL) to document best practices have identified a longer list of characteristics evident in best practices, in my experience four characteristics are particularly evident in all successful and well-developed programs of information literacy.

1. *Recognition by campus leadership that information literacy is a learning issue not a library issue and that classroom faculty must be responsible for students acquiring information literacy abilities.* In some ways this is the hardest to accomplish. Many librarians are reluctant to relinquish this responsibility, and in many cases what is being sold as information literacy is not as yet clearly identifiable as part of the critical thinking skills needed for lifelong learning; indeed, in some cases the packaging still appears very like the library or bibliography instruction of earlier years. Few students will commit to learning anything beyond what their classroom faculty honor and require, so the active involvement of the latter is essential.

2. *Strong partnering among library and classroom faculty, which includes planning as well as implementation of information literacy programs.* This is clearly a case where the whole equals more than the sum of its parts. Classroom faculty bring the in-depth knowledge of the subject and a direct impact on students' interests; librarians bring the information expertise and knowledge of proven pedagogical approaches to the mastery of information literacy abilities. Together they create a winning combination where the winners are the students.

3. *Programs built on campus-determined student learning outcomes against which progress is assessed.* The Association of College and Research Libraries standards, which have been endorsed by the American Association of Higher Education (AAHE), make this quality indicator easier for all campuses. Because of the effort required and

for creditability purposes, standards and assessment practices are best developed at the national and system levels. It is important that campus standards have credibility based both on campus learning priorities and in these larger efforts. Moreover, having the ACRL standards endorsed by the AAHE is well worth calling attention to as protection against the "library issue" challenge addressed earlier.

4. *Information literacy programs institutionalized across the curriculum.* Even among campuses which are no longer characterized by one-shot information literacy sessions early in the semester, few can, as yet, boast that all their students have sufficient opportunities to master the full range of information literacy abilities they will need for effective lifelong learning. This learning is too important for a hit or miss approach or for an approach that is based on individually built relationships between librarians and classroom faculty. Rather there needs to be departmental or college-wide planning for strategic integration of learning initiatives that build on and reinforce each other.

In some ways this book is being written both at the best and worst of times for the expansion and enhancement of information literacy programs. It is the best of times because the emphasis on student learning outcomes, which are needed in the after-graduation real world, provides a mandate for information literacy. It is the worst of times as national and state budgets hold little but doom and gloom for higher education. Yet I always remember an observation made years ago when Frank Newman, long-time head of the Education Commission of the States, was president of Rhode Island University. Newman observed that history showed it was not in times of prosperity but in times of budget crises that higher education made its best steps forward. When we can't do business as usual, we are forced to be our most creative.

So it is both a joy and a responsibility to join with the academicians represented in this book to continue to make information literacy a priority and to use all our creativity to make a difference in the lives of current and future generations of students—students who, because of their efforts, will be well prepared for lifelong learning in today's Information Society.

Patricia Senn Breivik
Dean, San Jose State University Library and
Chair of the National Forum on Information Literacy

Preface

The purpose of this book is to showcase practical examples of how information literacy programs and partnerships can transform the higher education teaching and learning environments.

Information literacy is no longer just a library issue, an education issue, or an American issue. In this era of the global economy, countries around the world are recognizing that an educated, skilled, and information-literate society is necessary for economic productivity and societal well being. Individuals who are knowledgeable about finding, evaluating, analyzing, integrating, managing, and conveying information effectively and efficiently are held in high esteem as being information competent. They are the students, colleagues, workers, and citizens who are most successful at finding solutions to problems and producing new ideas and directions for the future.

Colleges and universities have the responsibility for providing students with the opportunities to develop information competence skills and abilities. The contributors to this book, each an expert in the field, address various practices of information literacy at two-year and four-year institutions, looking at issues from a practical point of view.

Review of Contents

The Introduction discusses why information literacy programs are important by looking at the current information environment, clarifying differences between information literacy and computer literacy, pointing out the needs of the business community, and noting the inclusion of information literacy in revised accreditation documents. The Introduction also suggests components for an information literacy curriculum and supports the notion of university outreach and partnership programs, especially with local high schools and community colleges.

The topic of partnerships is expanded in Chapter One, which offers various models for developing faculty-librarian partnerships on the campus. Chapter Two suggests collaborative strategies and successful models for embedding information literacy into the higher education curriculum, with particular attention to programs of teacher education, the first-year experience, residential learning communities, writing across the curriculum, faculty development, service learning, and on-line or distance education. Chapter Three reviews current practices for establishing and creating interactive tutorials that can be easily integrated into a variety of courses in order to help freshman students develop their information literacy skills. Chapter Four details the conceptualization, development, and implementation of an undergraduate interdisciplinary program in the humanities. Library faculty and faculty members in the academic disciplines have collaborated on the program, carefully aligning information literacy learning outcomes with course requirements.

Chapter Five addresses the special needs of research institutions, discussing the challenges these complex institutions face in establishing, nurturing, and integrating an information literacy program within the curriculum. Chapter Six looks at how an assessment instrument can be created to consistently measure information literacy learning outcomes across multiple institutions at the community college level. Chapter Seven extends the conversation on assessment by showing how the information literacy skills of under-graduate students can be measured within a university setting.

The Conclusion provides a distillation of key points for continuing the dialogue on information literacy in the future. Readers will find each chapter to be of keen interest, and each can stand on its own; chapters need not be read sequentially.

Audience

This book will be of particular interest to the following groups:

- Faculty members and department chairs involved with curriculum decisions, course articulation, assessment projects, development and coordination of general education courses, or establishment of first-year learning communities

- Faculty members involved with professional preparation programs, such as teacher education

- Researchers investigating effective teaching and learning practices among higher education institutions

- Academic librarians involved with campus teaching, technology, curriculum, or assessment activities

- Administrators charged with curricular program planning and review

- Directors of faculty development centers interested in reaching out to both part-time and full-time faculty members

- Assessment coordinators who are looking at how embedded skills, knowledge, and abilities can coalesce or enhance student performance

- Faculty and others involved with campus teaching and learning and technology issues

- Information technology and media services personnel who help faculty members improve the effectiveness of their Web-based courses

- Student affairs professionals who provide leadership for living/learning communities and outreach programs to secondary schools and community colleges

All will gain valuable information, and working together can ensure that students graduate with a mastery of information competence.

Acknowledgments

Many individuals have helped to develop, improve, and encourage this publication. Particular appreciation is extended to library faculty and management colleagues, discipline-based teaching and research faculty, and academic affairs administrators. All have been generous with their time and more than willing to share their ideas, experiences, and expertise. To each, I am most grateful.

Hayward, California   ILENE F. ROCKMAN
January 2004

The Authors

Pam Baker has been a member of the library faculty at California State University (CSU) Monterey Bay since 1997 and coordinator of library instruction since 1999. As coordinator, she is the primary faculty liaison for campuswide information competence instruction and library liaison to the CSU Monterey Bay information competency project with the Human Communications Institute. She is responsible for all lower-division, course-integrated information competence instruction and codevelops and coteaches CST 101, the principal course that fulfills the technology and information competence university learning requirement. She is current chair of CSU Monterey Bay's university-wide Technology/Information University Learning Requirement Committee. In 2002, she was chair of the California Clearinghouse for Library Instruction and responsible for planning the group's spring workshop "Redefining and Redesigning Library Instruction."

Patricia Senn Breivik serves as dean of the Dr. Martin Luther King, Jr. Library at San Jose State University, where, in collaboration with the San Jose Public Library, a new joint library opened in 2003. She has also served as library dean at Wayne State University in Detroit; associate vice president for information resources at the Towson State University campus of the University of Maryland system;

director of library and telecommunications services, which supported three academic institutions on the Auraria campus in Denver; dean of library services at Sangamon State University in Springfield, Illinois; and assistant dean of Pratt Institute in the Graduate School of Library and Information Science in Brooklyn, New York. She serves as chair of the National Forum on Information Literacy, is a past president of the Association of College and Research Libraries, and is a frequent speaker and writer on the topic of information literacy and resource-based learning. Her awards and honors include the Miriam Dudley Instruction Librarian Award from the Association of College and Research Libraries (1997), the Pratt Institute Alumni Achievement Award (1995), the American Association of School Librarians Executive Board recognition for special contributions to school library media programs (1992), the American Council on Education Fellows Program in Academic Administration Service Award (1990), and the Columbia University School of Library Service Distinguished Alumni Award (1989).

Amelie Brown has worked as a reference librarian at California State University, Hayward, and Golden Gate University in San Francisco. She has been reference and instruction librarian at Diablo Valley College in northern California since 1999. She has developed information competency instruction programs and materials, including a workbook for developmental students and a series of workshops. She has initiated learning communities and has taught courses in basic library and research skills. She has also collaborated on the development of specific information competency learning outcomes and an accompanying proficiency exam for the California Community Colleges.

Lynn Cameron is coordinator of library instruction at James Madison University (JMU) in Virginia, where she has been involved in assessment of information literacy since the late 1980s. As a member of JMU's General Education Committee, she played an active role in integrating information literacy with the curriculum and implementing a required competency test. As a result of these efforts, the university's information literacy program was selected as a Best Practices program in 2002 by the Association of College and Research Libraries. In addition to coordinating instruction, she serves as the liaison librarian for psychology and geography. She also has made presentations on assessment at various higher education conferences.

Renée R. Curry has been an English professor in the California State University (CSU) system for thirteen years. She spent ten of those years at CSU San Marcos and the last three years at CSU Monterey Bay. She is currently director of the Institute for Human Communication at Monterey Bay. Her involvement with library faculty in information competency work at both campuses has been ongoing since 1995. In addition to her work with information competency, her research, teaching, and writing address assessment practices across the curriculum, as well as issues in poetry, fiction, and film studies. But her favorite work is that of teaching and learning in the university classroom. In the past thirteen years, she has taught more than seventy lower-division, upper-division, and graduate courses.

Susan Carol Curzon is dean of the Delmar T. Oviatt Library at California State University (CSU), Northridge, and has also served as director of libraries for the City of Glendale, California, and held senior administrative library positions with the County of Los Angeles Public Library. Her honors and awards include Administrator of the Year from the student body of CSU Northridge in 1996; Distinguished Alumna from the University of California, Riverside, in 1994; and Librarian of the Year from *Library Journal* in 1993. From 1995 to 2002, she was the chair of California State University's Information Competence Committee, which has developed an information literacy program at all twenty-three CSU campuses as well as a systemwide assessment of student information competence skills.

Trudi E. Jacobson has been coordinator of user education programs at the University at Albany since 1990. Previously, she was the reference services coordinator at Siena College in New York state. She has written numerous articles about information literacy and user education, has taught the user education graduate course at the School of Information Science and Policy at the University of Albany, and in 1998 received its Distinguished Alumni Award. She has served as chair of the Instruction Section of the Association of College and Research Libraries and is a member of the editorial board of *Research Strategies*.

Bonnie Gratch Lindauer has worked for twenty-five years in all types of academic libraries and has been active in the Association of College and Research Libraries, serving on various committees, including the Information Literacy Task Force and the Executive Board of the Institute for Information Literacy. She has published numerous articles, book chapters, and books on reference service evaluation, assessment of library research skills, and institutional outcomes assessment. Her recent publications include the award-winning article "Defining and Measuring the Library's Impact on Campuswide Outcomes," published in the November 1998 issue of *College and Research Libraries*; "Measuring What Matters: An Outcomes Assessment Manual for Library and Learning Resource Centers," published in 2000 by the Library and Learning Resources Association of the California Community Colleges; and "Comparing the Regional Accreditation Standards: Outcomes Assessment and Other Trends," published in the January–March 2002 issue of the *Journal of Academic Librarianship*.

Ilene F. Rockman is manager of the Information Competence Initiative for the Office of the Chancellor of the California State University, the largest system of higher education in North America. Formerly the interim dean of library services at California Polytechnic State University, San Luis Obispo, and the deputy university librarian at California State University, Hayward, she has taught information literacy credit courses at two-year and four-year institutions, has developed summer information literacy workshops for faculty members, and is a popular author and speaker on these topics. Her honors and awards include the Distinguished Librarian Award from the Education and Behavioral Sciences Section of the Association of College and Research Libraries (2003), the Literati Award for Excellence from MCB University Press of the United Kingdom (2001), the Exemplary Service Award from the California Reading Association (1992), and the Professional Development Liaison Award from the Association of College and Research Libraries (1991). Since 1986, she has served as the editor-in-chief of *Reference Services Review*, a quarterly, peer-reviewed international journal that focuses on reference and instructional services for libraries in the digital age.

Patrick Sullivan is currently a reference and instruction librarian at San Diego State University, where he works with both undergraduate and graduate students. He was formerly the interim coordinator of library instruction at San Diego State University. He has also worked as a reference and instruction librarian at California Polytechnic State University, San Luis Obispo, where he was involved with information literacy initiatives, and as the evening MBA librarian at the University of California, Berkeley. He has taught credit-bearing information literacy courses and has given conference presentations on the creation and development of information literacy tutorials. At San Diego State University, he and his colleagues received an information competence grant from the California State University to develop Web-based information literacy tutorials for use with freshman students.

Integrating Information Literacy into the Higher Education Curriculum

Introduction: The Importance of Information Literacy

Ilene F. Rockman

Information literacy is no longer just a library issue. It is *the* critical campuswide issue for the twenty-first century, of keen importance to all educational stakeholders, including administrators, faculty, librarians, media and information technologists, assessment coordinators, faculty development directors, service learning specialists, student affairs personnel, and career development professionals. Broadly defined, information literacy is a set of abilities that allow a person to recognize when information is needed and to effectively and efficiently act on that need.

Why is information literacy important? The increasingly complex world in which we live now contains an abundance of information choices—print, electronic, image, spatial, sound, visual, and numeric. The issue is no longer one of not having enough information; it is just the opposite—too much information, in various formats and not all of equal value. In a time of more than 17 million Internet sites, three billion Web pages, and more than a million items in a typical medium-sized academic library, the ability to act confidently (and not be paralyzed by information overload) is critical to academic success and personal self-directed learning.

Lorie Roth aptly describes the current information environment and the pitfalls facing college and university students: "With the explosion of information generated and stored, the unregulated sprawl of the Internet, the shift from a print- to an image-based culture, the development of sound and video archives, and the ease of seemingly infinite reproduction of words and pictures through electronic media, the pitfalls for college students have multiplied geometrically. There is so much information, so much of it of doubtful quality, so accessible through so many different platforms" (Roth, 1999, p. 42).

Individuals who are knowledgeable about finding, evaluating, analyzing, integrating, managing, and conveying information to others efficiently and effectively are held in high esteem. These are the students, workers, and citizens who are most successful at solving problems, providing solutions, and producing new ideas and directions for the future. They are lifelong learners.

Today's students, then, can benefit throughout their lives from learning a process for becoming information literate—that is, acquiring the skills required to intelligently and systematically find, interpret, select, evaluate, organize, and use information for a specific purpose.

Within the college or university environment, it is also important for students to be able to build upon the foundation of information literacy knowledge by successfully transferring this learning from course to course, understanding the critical and empowering role of information in a free and democratic society, and demonstrating ethical behavior and academic integrity as consumers, as well as producers, of information.

Ernest Boyer recognized that facilitating that empowering role of information is an important goal of education. In 1994, he stated that "information is, in fact, our most precious resource. In such a world, education should empower everyone, not the few. But for information to become *knowledge*, and ultimately, one hopes, *wisdom*, it must be organized. And, in this new climate, the *public* interest challenge, beyond access and equity is, I believe, sorting and selection. The challenge of educators is to help students make sense of a world described by some as 'information overload'" (Boyer, 1997, p. 140).

It was also noted several years later by the Boyer Commission on Educating Undergraduates in the Research University that "undergraduate education should be designed as a continuum that prepares students for continued learning and professional work through developing their talents to formulate questions and seek answers" (Boyer Commission on Educating Undergraduates in the Research University, 2001, p. 18). Information literacy is a key component for doing so.

What Is Information Literacy?

It is not uncommon to think of information literacy as the fusion or integration of library literacy, computer literacy, media literacy, technological literacy, critical thinking, ethics, and communication skills (Work Group on Information Competence, 1995).

The Information Competency Standards for Higher Education, produced by the Association of College and Research Libraries, notes that information literacy forms the basis for lifelong learning, is common to all disciplines, to all learning environments, and to all levels of education. It enables learners to master content, become self-directed learners, and assume greater control over their own learning. An information-literate individual is able to

- Determine the extent of information needed

- Access the needed information effectively and efficiently

- Evaluate information and its sources critically

- Incorporate selected information into his or her knowledge base

- Use information effectively to accomplish a specific purpose

- Understand the economic, legal, and social issues surrounding the use of information, and access and use information ethically and legally

(http://www.ala.org/Content/NavigationMenu/ACRL/
Standards_and_Guidelines/Information_Literacy_
Competency_Standards_for_Higher_Education.htm).

Evolution of Information Literacy

Is information literacy a new concept? In actuality, we can trace the origins of information literacy back to hundreds of years ago. Some accounts state that it originated with early library instruction courses in the nineteenth century (Grassian and Kaplowitz, 2001, p. 14), while others trace it to the beginning of the twentieth century (Evans, 1914). In 1956, Patricia Knapp posited the notion that library instruction should be a central component of a student's college experiences, stating that "Competence in library use, like competence in reading, is clearly not a skill to be acquired once and for all at any one given level in any one given course. It is, rather, a complex of knowledge, skills, and attitudes which must be developed over a period of time through repeated and varied experiences in the use of library resources" (Knapp, 1956, p. 224).

Faculty-librarian partnerships have been a salient component of such information literacy programs for the past several decades. In the 1970s, such collaborations included partnerships to develop competence in the use of the library for research purposes (Farber, 1974); partnerships to integrate library instruction into discipline courses (Dittmar, 1977); and partnerships to develop a yearlong integrated group of core courses for first-year students, including a library research course, to assist in the retention of underrepresented students (Rockman, 1978).

We can also look to 1989, the year of the American Library Association's Presidential Committee on Information Literacy, chaired by Patricia Senn Breivik, as a turning point in the visibility and advancement of information literacy just at a time when on-line information resources were becoming prevalent on most college and university campuses. The committee issued a final report that identified information literacy "as a survival skill in the information age," noting that "information literate people are those who have learned how to learn. They are people prepared for lifelong learning, because they can always find the information needed for any task or decision at hand." In addition, the report asserted that "people who are information literate—who know how to acquire knowledge and use it—are America's most valuable resource" (American Library Association, Presidential Committee on Information Literacy, 1989).

The following year, 1990, Breivik founded the National Forum on Information Literacy, a coalition of over ninety business, education, technology, media, and other organizations, to raise awareness of and share new developments in information literacy among K–12 and higher education, government offices, the business and workforce communities, and international constituencies. The forum meets several times a year in Washington, D.C., and pursues activities that examine the role of information in society. The forum supports, initiates, and monitors information literacy projects both in the United States and abroad; actively encourages the creation and adoption of information literacy guidelines; and works with teacher education programs to ensure that those new to the profession are able to incorporate information literacy into their teaching. All of these activities are committed to empowering individuals with the skills they need to function successfully in the Information Age (National Forum on Information Literacy, n.d.).

Several years later, in 1995, the California State University (CSU), the largest system of higher education in North America, with twenty-three campuses, over 400,000 students, and 44,000 faculty and staff members, created its Information Competence Initiative (http://www.calstate.edu/LS/infocomp.shtml) under the leadership of Susan Curzon of California State University, Northridge. The initiative was designed to help faculty and students think differently about how information is located, managed, evaluated, and used. Efforts resulted in the development of an information literacy presence on each of the twenty-three CSU campuses, the development of course-integrated and Web-based interactive instructional tutorials on information literacy. and summer faculty development workshops to help professors rethink and revise their assignment and curricular offerings. In addition, the initiative facilitated outreach efforts to high schools and community colleges to assist students in their transition to the university and help them succeed academically in their classes, support for a campus online information competence graduation requirement, the creation of various information literacy courses at the undergraduate and graduate levels, the integration of information competence principles into the learning outcomes of academic disciplines, and the assessment of student information competence skills and abilities.

In 2000, the Association of College and Research Libraries issued a landmark document, *Information Literacy Competency Standards for Higher Education*, which included performance indicators and learning outcomes that could be used to assess student progress (Association of College and Research Libraries, 2000). This document has had widespread influence on colleges and universities across the nation, as well as internationally, with translations into Spanish and Greek. A year after its publication, it was endorsed by the American Association for Higher Education.

Information literacy is not a concept limited to the United States. The International Federation of Library Associations and Institutions has an organizational section devoted to information literacy, which brings together librarians from around the world. The topic is of keen interest to educators in Canada, Australia, New Zealand, the United Kingdom, Europe, Scandinavia, Latin America, Mexico, Asia, and Africa (Rader, 1996; Bruce, Candy, and Klaus, 2000). In 2002, the First International Conference on Information Technology and Information Literacy was held, further increasing the visibility of information literacy in higher education around the world (http://www.iteu.gla.ac.uk/elit/itilit2002/index.html).

Information Literacy, Computer Literacy, and Information Technology

Computer ownership does not guarantee information literacy; students can use information technology to manipulate data and create documents without demonstrating information literacy skills. One cannot discount the enormous impact that technology has had in transforming the educational landscape in the past several decades and in making information easier to access, but technology alone does not make one information literate.

Shapiro and Hughes (1996) recognize and point out the differences between information literacy and computer use, noting, "Information and computer literacy, in the conventional sense, are functionally valuable technical skills. But information literacy should in fact be conceived more broadly as a new liberal art that extends from knowing how to use computers and access information to critical reflection on the nature of information itself, its technical infrastructure, and its social, cultural and even philosophical context and impact—as essential to the mental framework of the educated information-age citizen as the trivium of basic liberal arts (grammar, logic and rhetoric) was to the educated person in medieval society."

The National Research Council also discussed information literacy and information technology in the 1999 document *Being Fluent with Information Technology*. The report states:

> Information literacy focuses on content and communication: it encompasses authoring, information finding and organization, research, and information analysis, assessment, and evaluation. Content can take many forms: text, images, video, computer simulations, and multimedia interactive works. Content can also serve many purposes: news, art, entertainment, education, research and

scholarship, advertising, politics, commerce, and documents and records that structure activities of everyday
business and personal life. Information literacy subsumes
but goes far beyond the traditional textual literacy that
has been considered part of a basic education (the ability to read, write, and critically analyze various forms of
primarily textual literary works or personal and business
documents). By contrast, FITness focuses on a set of intellectual capabilities, conceptual knowledge, and contemporary skills associated with information technology.
. . . Both information literacy and FITness are essential
for individuals to use information technology effectively.
[National Research Council, 1999, pp. 48–50]

Several prominent individuals from the worlds of finance and
commerce have also recognized the value of information literacy.
Anthony Comper, president of the Bank of Montreal, told the 1999
graduating class at the University of Toronto that information literacy is essential to future success: "Whatever else you bring to the 21st
century workplace, however great your technical skills and however
attractive your attitude and however deep your commitment to excellence, the bottom line is that to be successful, you need to acquire a
high level of information literacy. What we need in the knowledge
industries are people who know how to absorb and analyze and integrate and create and effectively convey information—and who know
how to use information to bring real value to everything they under-
take." ("Information Literacy Key to Success . . . ," 1999).

Taizo Nishimura, former president, now retired, of the Toshiba
Corporation adds, "Information literacy is the ability to solve problems, taking advantage of information technology and networks.
Information literacy is not a new concept, rather a traditional one
in terms of problem solving" (Nishimura, 1999).

Terry Crane, former vice president for education products at
America Online, states, "Young people need a baseline of commu-

nication, analytical, and technical skills. We are no longer teaching about technology, but about information literacy—which is a process of turning information into meaning, understanding, and new ideas. Students need the thinking, reasoning, and civic abilities that enable them to succeed in—and ultimately lead—a contemporary democratic economy, workforce, and society" (Sanford, 2000).

There is also evidence that as various sectors of the corporate world embrace the principles of information literacy, information literacy concepts are being recognized as "new economy" skills (O'Sullivan, 2002). The move to a knowledge-based economy has revealed that many workers are poorly equipped to effectively use and manage information on a daily basis, lacking the ability to locate relevant information, critically analyze and assess its value and authority, and present it within legal and ethical parameters. Such situations can negatively affect the ability of businesses to compete and grow in a global economy, and of governments to prosper with increased revenues from businesses and corporations. It is for this reason that programs such as The Information Literacy Guidelines Business Plan, funded by the State of California's Technology, Trade, and Commerce Agency, were developed (Great Valley Center, 2002). The plan is intended to help all of the educational, community, and economic development organizations in the San Joaquin Valley of California develop a base of information-literate "knowledge workers," thus attracting employers to stimulate the economy.

Information Literacy and Higher Education

Why is information literacy important to higher education? Studies have shown that students are entering college and university environments without fundamental research and information competence skills (for example, the ability to formulate a research question, then efficiently and effectively find, evaluate, synthesize, and ethically use information pertaining to that question).

Students may have picked up the skills to send electronic mail, chat, and download music, but many have not learned how to effectively locate information; evaluate, synthesize, and integrate ideas; use information in original work or give proper credit for information used. Moreover, faculty want to see an improvement in the quality of student work, and students want to become more confident in their ability to complete assignments, carry out research projects, and become active, independent learners.

In addition, information literacy is required by accreditation organizations, expected by employers in the workplace for organizational success, and desired by society, which needs an informed citizenry that is capable of making well-reasoned and well-founded decisions.

The Western Association of Schools and Colleges, in its *Handbook of Accreditation* (2001, Standard 2, p. 20), notes that "baccalaureate programs engage students in an integrated course of study of sufficient breadth and depth to prepare them for work, citizenship, and a fulfilling life. These programs also ensure the development of core learning abilities and competencies including, but not limited to, college-level written and oral communication; college-level quantitative skills; information literacy; and the habit of critical analysis of data and argument."

The Middle States Commission on Higher Education has recognized the importance of information literacy by including it in "Characteristics of Excellence in Higher Education: Eligibility Requirements and Standards for Accreditation" (2002). Standard 11, "Educational Offerings," states, "Information literacy is an intellectual framework for identifying, finding, understanding, evaluating, and using information. Higher education has available a variety of new information resources and an evolving array of information technology and access structures, including computers, software applications, and databases, that supplement its print-based knowledge resources and present new complexities for teachers and learners. How to develop and utilize knowledge and skills and discipline-specific investigative methods to identify, access, retrieve, and apply relevant content is a challenge for the future of learning and teaching in our universities, colleges, and schools." Standard 12, "General Education" asserts, "The institution's curricula are designed so that students acquire and demonstrate college-level proficiency in general education and essential skills, including oral and written communication, scientific and quantitative reasoning, critical analysis and reasoning, technological competency, and information literacy."

The New England Association of Schools and Colleges now recognizes information literacy as a student learning outcome in its accreditation standards. Standard 7.4 notes, "Professionally qualified and numerically adequate staff administer the institution's library, information resources, and services. The institution includes appropriate orientation and training for use of these resources, as well as instruction in basic information literacy" (New England Association of Schools and Colleges, 2001, p. 19).

The National Council for the Accreditation of Teacher Education, in its "Professional Standards for the Accreditation of Schools, Colleges, and Departments of Education" (2001, p. 19), indicates, "teacher education candidates should be able to appropriately and effectively integrate technology and information literacy in instruction to support student learning."

The American Psychological Association's Board of Educational Affairs recognizes information literacy as a specific learning objective for undergraduate students (Murray, 2002) and notes in its learning goals, "students will demonstrate information competence and the ability to use computers and other technology for many purposes," including the demonstration of competent, ethical, and responsible use of information in academic work (American Psychological Association, 2000, p. 14).

The American Chemical Society (2002) states, "a student who intends to become a practicing chemist, or who will use chemistry in allied fields of science and medicine, should know how to use the chemical literature effectively and efficiently." Instruction can be achieved in several ways—for example, through a course dedicated to the subject of chemical information retrieval, which can be enhanced with focused library assignments; through integrating this skill into other chemistry courses, such as laboratory courses; and through discussions held in seminar courses.

"Standards for the English Language Arts," formulated by the National Council of Teachers of English and the International Reading Association (2001), states, "Students conduct research on issues and interests by generating ideas and questions, and by posing problems. They gather, evaluate, and synthesize data from a variety of sources (e.g., print and non-print texts, artifacts, people) to communicate their discoveries in ways that suit their purpose and audience. Students use a variety of technological and information resources (e.g., libraries, databases, computer networks, video) to gather and synthesize information and to create and communicate knowledge."

Just as accreditation bodies have recognized the value of information literacy, so have employers who have a vested interested in the competencies of college and university graduates. In *Information Literacy and Workplace Performance*, Tom Goad (2002) notes, "Information literacy—the ability to recognize the need for information, to locate, access, select, and apply it—was once an academic matter. Nowadays, the critical array of skills concerns anyone working in a knowledge-based environment."

This theme had resonated over a decade earlier in the list of critical skills developed by the Secretary of Labor's Commission on Achieving Necessary Skills (SCANS) (U.S Department of Labor, 1991). The commission challenged the American educational system, from preschools to postgraduate institutions, to focus on the skills and competencies that graduates need in order to be a successful part of a highly skilled workforce in a high-performance, information- and service-based economy.

The SCANS report, intended to help educators restructure curriculum and instruction, was intentionally titled "What Work

Requires of Schools." It specifically outlined the skills needed by competent individuals in a high-performance workplace: literacy; use of technology; critical thinking; problem solving; decision mak-ing; knowing how to learn; reasoning; and the ability to manage resources, work productively with others, acquire and evaluate information effectively, organize and maintain information, interpret and communicate information, and work with a variety of technologies.

Why should colleges and universities pay attention to the SCANS report and specifically to information skills and competencies? Although these competencies can be learned, they "must be taught and practiced, not merely absorbed as a result of unplanned academic experience" (Wingspread Group on Higher Education, 1993, p. 14). Several recent higher education reports and studies indicate that additional attention must be paid to information literacy skills, because today's college and university students still need assistance in developing and strengthening these important skills.

The May–June 2001 issue of *Change* magazine, published by the American Association for Higher Education, includes a study conducted by the National Center for Postsecondary Improvement entitled, "A Report to Stakeholders on the Conditions and Effectiveness of Postsecondary Education." This report notes that "less than half (48% of those students surveyed), feel confident in their ability to find information—essentially, in the skills needed to research a topic" (National Center for Postsecondary Improvement, 2001, p. 29).

These findings are supported by the Online Computer Library Center (2002) in the "OCLC White Paper on the Information Habits of College Students." This study reports that "more than 31% of all respondents use Internet search engines to find answers to their questions. However, people who use Internet search engines express frustration because they estimate that half of their searches are unsuccessful."

Leigh Watson Healy, vice president and chief analyst at Outsell, Inc., reported at the EDUCAUSE 2002 conference that two of the top information problems are "having enough time and knowing what's available" (Healy, 2002).

It is clear that the digital environment influences how students search for information and poses complex challenges for them in becoming information literate. A particular challenge for today's students is understanding the relationships between types of information resources, how to evaluate the appropriateness and reliability of these resources, and how to make intelligent choices among them.

The Pew Internet and American Life Project (Lenhart, Simon, and Graziano, 2001) notes, "for many teens, the Internet has replaced the library as the primary tool for doing research." Another Pew study elaborated on this concept, reporting that "many students are likely to use information found on search engines and various web sites as research material. . . . A great challenge for today's colleges is how to teach students search techniques that will get them to the information they want, and how to evaluate it" (Jones, 2002).

California State University's information literacy assessment studies, conducted in 2000 and 2001, provide rich data about student search behavior patterns, based on audiotaped and videotaped focus group conversations, ethnographic field notes, participant observations, keystroke patterns recorded by screen capture software, questionnaires, open-ended essays, and artifacts used by students (for example, disks, notebooks). The studies also used anthropological and sociological methodologies. Evidence indicates that students are entering the California State University without core information literacy skills and abilities such as critical thinking, decision making, and self-directed learning. This multidimensional qualitative research study also finds that students tend to exhibit an overreliance on Web-based information resources and sources found through search engines, as opposed to other sources such as information found in library catalogues and subscription databases. In addition, students often search using keywords rather than controlled vocabulary terms. A keyword search retrieves information from anywhere in the record; a controlled vocabulary search uses subject terms (often from a thesaurus), so the retrieval is likely to be more relevant. Thus, they often miss important sources of information. They often do not make distinctions between scholarly and popular works, and they tend to embrace the World Wide Web over the traditional library because of convenience, flexibility, and access to what is perceived to be large amounts of current information. As a result, students may run the risk of accepting whatever information is displayed from a search engine, placing greater value on current sources of information than on the more in-depth discussions that are often found in books (California State University Information Competence Assessment, 2002).

These experiences are consistent with those reported in other studies, which indicate that students "are leaving [the] university without the necessary transferable skills to cope in an information based society" (Ray and Day, 1998); do not display "a high level of information competence" and "at best . . . possess sporadic knowledge" (Caravello, Borah, Herschman, and Mitchell, 2001); and "think they know more about accessing information and conducting library research than they are able to demonstrate when put to the test" (Maughan, 2002).

Yet there are some bright moments that demonstrate how students can improve their grades when engaged with information competence principles through participation in cohesive, library-sponsored hands-on workshops and courses.

The institutional research unit of Glendale Community College (http://www.glendale.edu/library/icimproves.htm), a two-year institution in Southern California, recently reported a positive relationship between student participation in a semester-long information competency course and grades in other courses. The results of the longitudinal study indicate that information competency instruction has had a significant impact on student success (Moore, Brewster, Dorroh, and Moreau, 2002).

Such formal information literacy instruction by librarians or faculty members is important to include in the curriculum for several reasons. Content mastered by graduation is soon outdated or forgotten by students. Learning must continue beyond the time spent in earning a degree. To develop competence in an area of inquiry, students must have a deep foundation of factual knowledge; understand facts and ideas in the context of a conceptual framework; and organize knowledge in ways that facilitate retrieval and application (Donovan, Bransford, and Pellegrino, 1999, p. 12).

It is clear from the studies that students are not picking up information literacy skills on their own. Without a concerted instructional effort that gives students multiple opportunities to practice their information literacy skills, such skills will not be effectively developed. Just as an athlete needs sustained conditioning and practice before a big game and a musician needs to rehearse before a major performance, a student needs multiple experiences to practice and hone information literacy skills before graduating and pursuing advanced study or entering the workplace.

Information Literacy Curriculum

So, what does an information literacy curriculum look like? It is campuswide; problem-based, inquiry-based, and resource-based (that is, it uses a variety of information resources); makes effective use of instructional pedagogies and technologies; is learner-centered; and is integrated and articulated with a discipline's learning outcomes. It enhances and expands student learning through a coherent, systematic approach that facilitates the transfer of learning across the curriculum.

The Boyer Commission on Educating Undergraduates in the Research University called for a first-year experience to provide stimulation for "intellectual growth and a firm grounding in inquiry-based learning" (2001, p. 12). Information literacy fits well with this educational goal.

Ideally, a student is introduced to information literacy at the beginning of his or her freshman year in a required course such as "Introduction to University Life," "Expository Writing and Research," or "Technology and Information." It is even better if the student learns about information literacy principles in a course, such as "Fundamentals of Information Literacy," that is linked to a freshman learning community, with library assignments aligned with assignments in other courses.

The student continues to encounter information literacy opportunities throughout the curriculum, both vertically (within the major) and horizontally (across the curriculum), in both lower- and upper-division general education, elective, prerequisite, pre-professional, and major courses, culminating in a senior capstone experience in which such information literacy skills can be demonstrated in the classroom, the laboratory, the field, the performing arts center, or elsewhere through creative or research activities.

Including information literacy in general education courses is a key strategy for closing the gap across curricular boundaries, because general education courses form the foundation of a common learning experience for all students. Such courses help students to make intellectual connections between disciplines, solve problems, and think deeply, independently, and critically outside of their major areas of study. Some institutions have successfully included information literacy experiences as an integrated component of a lower-division general education program (Sonntag and Ohr, 1996; Faust, 2001). Benefits to students in such a model include those reported by a sophomore business major after completing the Fundamentals of Information Literacy class as one of her lower-division general education requirements: "I was lost before I took this class" ("Newsletter of the California State University Libraries," 2002, p. 4).

For transfer and graduate students, information literacy principles can be integrated into transition courses, as well as into core research classes in the discipline.

At Minneapolis Community and Technical College, students seeking the Associate of Arts transfer degree are required to complete a two-unit information literacy course, "Information Literacy and Research Skills," taught by library faculty, which provides foundational information literacy knowledge and skills. After completing the course, students are better prepared for upper-division work (Eland, 2002). Graduate students can also benefit from gaining information literacy knowledge to help them successfully complete their research and writing requirements and better use their expertise to forge research connections within their academic disciplines.

Well-designed assignments are central to student learning, because they provide opportunities for active engagement with subject content, challenging students to think critically, reflect on their processes for finding and using information, and take the necessary steps to take charge of their own learning.

Library and discipline faculty can work together to create assignments that demonstrate how well students have learned, applied, and communicated information literacy principles (for example, examination of case studies; analysis of open-ended problems; creation of class presentations, poster sessions, written reports, research logs, Web sites, or PowerPoint presentations; development of reflective essays or journal entries; or presentation of examples of how published research can help to provide solutions in clinical settings).

In *Tools for Teaching*, Barbara Gross Davis suggests that assignments for first-year students be divided into sequential steps, with specific due dates and checkpoints for each piece—identifying a topic; stating the paper's title, purpose, and major points; gathering sources; developing an outline; writing the first draft; revising the paper; and submitting the final paper. Such activities help students to manage their time and work through the process of writing a paper. In addition, these steps provide opportunities for instructional intervention and reflect important components of information literacy. Collaborative partnerships between librarians and discipline faculty are essential to successfully develop these types of assignments.

Sustained partnerships between librarians and faculty development directors are also important in providing guidance and support to both full-time and part-time faculty members so that they have a consistent and critical understanding of the principles and pedagogy of information literacy.

Leora Baron, director of the Academy of the Art of Teaching at Florida International University in Miami, writes, "Learning to find your way through the information maze pays dividends for faculty and students alike. Faculty members quickly discover that becoming information literate has its rewards in increasing their ability to provide students with new and refined tools for academic success, and in expanding their own ability to refine and expand research activities" (Baron, 2001). Leadership provided by faculty development centers (workshops, seminars, and summer institutes on such topics as defining and assessing information literacy, preventing student plagiarism, integrating information literacy principles into course management and learning software packages such as WebCT and Blackboard, and effectively incorporating information literacy tutorials into course requirements) is critical for helping professors understand how to use and evaluate the outcomes of resource-, problem-, or inquiry-based instruction in support of campus information literacy goals.

Outreach Activities

Another important activity in advancing the information literacy agenda is for faculty and librarians to reach out to the elementary and secondary educational communities to ensure that students are introduced to information literacy principles prior to the start of their higher education academic careers. That is the intent of the Intersegmental Committee of the Academic Senates of the California Community Colleges, the California State University, and the University of California (2002). The committee's document, *Academic Literacy: A Statement of Competencies Expected of Students Entering California's Public Colleges and Universities*, produced by a faculty task force, notes the following:

- In order to be prepared for college and university courses, students need greater exposure to, and instruction in, academic literacy than they receive in English classes alone. This calls for greater co-ordination of literacy education among subject matter areas within high schools. [p. 3]

- Students' success in college has as much to do with their ability to find information as to recall it. [p. 6]

- While many entering students are familiar with some technological elements (notably e-mail and Web browsing), few demonstrate the critical ability to evaluate online resources. [p. 6]

Opportunities for university personnel to partner with elementary and secondary schools in the area of information literacy to help strengthen students' skills prior to entering colleges or universities are plentiful and just take time, imagination, resources, and commitment.

For example, the UCLA K–16 Collaborative was established in 1996 to reach out to the educational community surrounding the University of California at Los Angeles. As part of this key initiative, the UCLA College Library established its Information Literacy Instructional Pipeline Partnership project (Mitchell and Brasley, 2001). The project, developed by school and university library practitioners, resulted in a successful in-service development program for classroom teachers on the fundamentals of information literacy, the development of integrative lesson plans, and the creation of class activities and discipline-based curricular modules. All activities were intended to strengthen the information literacy skills of both the secondary students and their teachers.

In 1997, Rutgers University librarians, the chair of the university's education department, and high school teachers worked together in a yearlong partnership program to help students in an urban secondary school setting become more information literate.

The goals were to provide training in technology and information literacy skills through the university library to selected high school teachers, who would incorporate them into the high school curriculum and teach them to students, since students rarely receive intensive training in information literacy from a local school site (Calderhead, 1999, p. 336).

That same year, another collaborative partnership was formed among three campuses of the California State University (Dominguez Hills, Northridge, and San Marcos) and their surrounding local schools. Librarians at these institutions created a forum series for area high school teachers to help them better prepare secondary students to successfully complete the requirements demanded of a university education (http://library.csusm.edu/departments/ilp/ilp_projects/HiSc/ICHS.html). University librarians held sessions with local high school librarians to introduce them to a model information competence program, to share core information competencies that could be incorporated into the local secondary school curriculum, and to provide hands-on training sessions in finding, using, and evaluating electronic resources.

Other examples include librarians from the University of Colorado at Boulder who developed an outreach program to a secondary school in the foothills of the Rocky Mountains to provide active-learning, hands-on information literacy workshops for college-bound high school students (Gresham and Van Tassel, 1999), and personnel from Wayne State University (Nichols, 1999) and the University of Nebraska–Lincoln (Pearson and McNeil, 2002) who worked closely with their area high schools in a similar vein.

Why should university librarians reach out to the local educational communities to integrate information literacy competencies into curriculum and classroom instruction? Recent studies have pointed out that high school students lack information-seeking skills (Neuman, 1993; Nahl and Harada, 1996), while other studies have shown that quality library programs can positively affect student achievement (Hartzell, 2002). Research results from library impact studies in Alaska, Colorado, Iowa, New Mexico, Oregon, and Pennsylvania show that the school library makes a difference in student performance (Lance, 2002); it is in the best interest of university personnel to partner with neighboring local schools to ensure that students have the requisite information literacy skills, prior to beginning college or university studies, to be successful in their higher education academic and work careers.

Conclusion

This introduction has discussed the importance of integrating information literacy into the higher education curriculum through a campuswide approach, including various partnership models. Through collaborative alliances between library personnel and faculty, technologists, administrators, and other higher education professionals, students can develop a process for personal empowerment by becoming and remaining information literate throughout their lives.

This chapter has also emphasized that information literacy is more than computer literacy or the ability to use technology; instead, it is the ability to find, evaluate, analyze, integrate, communicate, and use information to solve problems, create new ideas, make informed decisions, and turn data into meaning. It is the responsibility of the entire college or university to help our students to become information literate, an essential element for future success.

References

American Chemical Society. "Chemical Information Retrieval." 2002. http://www.chemistry.org/portal/Chemistry?PID=acsdisplay.html&DOC= education%5Ccpt%5Cts_cheminfo.html. Accessed Jan. 2, 2003.

American Library Association, Presidential Committee on Information Literacy. "Final Report." 1989. http:// http://www.ala.org/Content/ NavigationMenu/ACRL/Publications/White_Papers_and_Reports/ Presidential_Committee_on_Information_Literacy.htm. Accessed Nov. 1, 2002.

American Psychological Association, Board of Educational Affairs. "Under-graduate Psychology Major Learning Goals and Outcomes: A Report." 2000. http://www.apa.org/ed/pcue/taskforcereport.pdf. Accessed Nov. 1, 2002.

Association of College and Research Libraries. *Information Literacy Competency Standards for Higher Education*. Chicago: Association of College and Research Libraries, 2000. Also available at http://www.ala.org/Content/ NavigationMenu/ACRL/Standards_and_Guidelines/Information_ Literacy_Competency_Standards_for_Higher_Education.htm. Accessed Nov. 1, 2002.

Baron, Leora. "Why Information Literacy: Empowering Teachers and Students in the Classroom and Beyond." *NEA Higher Education Advocate Online*, Aug. 2001. http://www.nea.org/he/advo01/advo0108/front.html. Accessed Nov. 19, 2002.

Boyer, Ernest L. "New Technologies and the Public Interest." In *Selected Speeches 1979–1995*. Princeton, N.J.: Carnegie Foundation for the Advancement of Teaching, 1997. pp. 137–142.

Boyer Commission on Educating Undergraduates in the Research University. "Reinventing Undergraduate Education: Three Years After the Boyer Report." 2001, p. 18. http://www.sunysb.edu/pres/0210066-Boyer%20Report%20Final.pdf.

Bruce, Christine, Philip Candy, and Kelmut Klaus (eds.). *Information Literacy Around the World: Advances in Programs and Research*. Wagga Wagga, New South Wales, Australia: Centre for Information Studies, Charles Sturt University, 2000.

Calderhead, Veronica. "Partnership in Electronic Learning." *Reference Services Review*, 1999, *27*(4), 336–343.

California State University. "Information Competence Assessment Phase Two Summary Report." 2002. http://www.csupomona.edu/~kkdunn/ Icassess/phase2summary.htm. Accessed Nov. 1, 2002.

California State University. "Information Competence Initiative." 2001. http://www.calstate.edu/LS/infocomp.shtml. Accessed Nov. 1, 2002.

Caravello, Patti S., Eloisa Gomez Borah, Judith Herschman, and Eleanor Mitchell. "UCLA Library Information Competence at UCLA: Report of a Survey Project." 2001. http://www.library.ucla.edu/infocompetence/ index_noframes.htm. Accessed Nov. 2, 2002.

Davis, Barbara Gross. *Tools for Teaching*. San Francisco: Jossey-Bass, 1993, p. 215.

Dittmar, Jeanne. "Library Service Enhancement Program, F. W. Crumb Memorial Library, State University College, Potsdam, New York. Final Report." Bethesda, Md.: ERIC Document Reproduction Service, 1977. (ED 157 554)

Donovan, M. Suzanne, John D. Bransford, and James W. Pellegrino (eds.). *How People Learn: Bridging Research and Practice.* Washington, D.C.: National Academy Press, 1999.

Eland, Tom. E-mail message posted to *ILI-Digest 122,* Dec. 24, 2002. [Available from ILI-l Mailing List Archive at http://bubl.ac.uk/mail/ilild/]

Evans, Henry Ridgely. *Library Instruction in Universities, Colleges, and Normal Schools.* Washington, D.C.: Government Printing Office, 1914.

Farber, Evan. "Library Instruction Throughout the Curriculum: Earlham College Program." In John Lubans (ed.). *Educating the Library User.* New York: Bowker, 1974, pp. 145–162.

Faust, Judith. "Teaching Information Literacy in 50 Minutes a Week: The CSUH Experience." *Journal of Southern Academic and Special Librarianship,* 2001, *21*(3). http://southernlibrarianship.icaap.org/content/v02n03/faust_j01.htm. Accessed Nov. 1, 2002.

Glendale Community College. "Information Competency Improves Grades." n.d. http://www.glendale.edu/library/icimproves.htm. Accessed Nov. 1, 2002.

Goad, Tom W. *Information Literacy and Workplace Performance.* Westport, Conn.: Quorum Books, 2002.

Grassian, Esther S., and Joan R. Kaplowitz. *Information Literacy Instruction: Theory and Practice.* New York: Neal-Schuman, 2001.

Great Valley Center. "Information Literacy Guidelines Business Plan: An Initiative of ACCESS II: Regional Connectivity Initiatives for the San Joaquin Valley, funded by the California Technology, Trade, and Commerce Agency, Division of Science, Technology, and Innovation." Unpublished document, Great Valley Center, Modesto, CA, Dec. 2002.

Gresham, Keith, and Debra Van Tassel. "Expanding the Learning Community: An Academic Library Outreach Program to High Schools." *Reference Librarian,* 1999, 67/68, 161–173.

Hartzell, Gary. "Capitalizing on the School Library's Potential to Positively Affect Student Achievement." 2002. http://www.imls.gov/pubs/whitehouse0602/Resources.pdf. Accessed Nov. 2, 2002.

Healy, Leigh Watson. "The Voice of the User: Where Students and Faculty Go for Information." 2002. http://www.educause.edu/ir/library/powerpoint/EDU0248c.pps. Accessed Nov. 15, 2002.

"Information Literacy Key to Success in 21st Century, Bank of Montreal CEO Advises University of Toronto Graduates." *Canada Newswire*, June 14, 1999. Available from ProQuest Information and Learning. Accessed Mar. 11, 2000.

Information Technology and Information Literacy 2002 Conference, University of Glasgow. http://www.iteu.gla.ac.uk/elit/itilit2002/index.html. [Selected papers appear in Martin, Allan, and Rader. *Information and IT Literacy: Enabling Learning in the 21st Century*. London: Facet Publishing, 2003.]

Intersegmental Committee of the Academic Senates of the California Community Colleges, the California State University, and the University of California. *Academic Literacy: A Statement of Competencies Expected of Students Entering California's Public Colleges and Universities*. Sacramento: Intersegmental Committee of the Academic Senates of the California Community Colleges, the California State University, and the University of California, Spring 2002. Also available at http://www.academicsenate.cc.ca.us/publications/papers/academicliteracy/main.htm.

Jones, Steve. "The Internet Goes to College: How Students are Living in the Future with Today's Technology." Sept. 15, 2002. Pew and American Life Project. http://www.pewinternet.org/reports/pdfs/PIP_College_Report.pdf. Accessed October 1, 2002.

Knapp, Patricia B. "A Suggested Program of College Instruction in the Use of the Library." *Library Trends*, 1956, 26(3), 224–231.

Lance, Keith Curry. "What Research Tells Us About the Importance of School Libraries." *Teacher Librarian*, special supplement, Oct. 2002, 39(1), 76–78.

Lenhart, Amanda, Maya Simon, and Mike Graziano. "The Internet and Education: Findings of the Pew Internet and American Life Project." Sept. 1, 2001. http://www.pewinternet.org/reports/toc.asp?Report=39. Accessed Sept. 10, 2001.

Maughan, Patricia D. "Assessing Information Literacy Among Undergraduates: A Discussion of the Literature and the University of California-Berkeley Assessment Experience." *College and Research Libraries*, 2002, 62(1), 71–85.

Middle States Commission on Higher Education. "Standard 11: Educational Offerings" and In "Characteristics of Excellence in Higher Education: Eligibility Requirements and Standards for Accreditation." Philadelphia, PA: Middle States Commission on Higher Education, 2002a, p. 32. http://www.msache.org/charac02.pdf. Accessed Nov. 1, 2002.

Middle States Commission on Higher Education. "Standard 12: General Education." In "Characteristics of Excellence in Higher Education: Eligibility

Requirements and Standards for Accreditation." Philadelphia, PA: Middle States Commission on Higher Education, 2002b. http://www. msache.org/charac02.pdf. Accessed Nov. 1, 2002.

Mitchell, Eleanor, and Stephanie Sterling Brasley. "Information Competency Continuum: A University, K–12 Collaboration." In Barbara I. Dewey (ed.). *Library User Education: Powerful Learning, Powerful Partnerships*. Lanham, Md.: Scarecrow Press, 2001, pp. 248–255.

Moore, Deborah, Steve Brewster, Cynthia Dorroh, and Michael Moreau. "Information Competency Instruction in a Two Year College: One Size Does Not Fit All." *Reference Services Review*, 2002, *30*(4), 300–306.

Murray, Bridget. "What Psych Majors Need to Know." *Monitor on Psychology*, July–Aug. 2002, *33*(7). http://www.apa.org/monitor/julaug02/psychmajors. html. Accessed Nov. 1, 2002.

Nahl, Diane, and Violet Harada. "Composing Boolean Search Statements: Self Confidence, Content Analysis, Search Logic, and Errors." *School Library Media Quarterly*, 1996, *24*, 199–207.

National Center for Postsecondary Improvement. "A Report to Stakeholders on the Condition and Effectiveness of Postsecondary Education." *Change*, May–June 2001, *33*(3), 27–42.

National Council for the Accreditation of Teacher Education. "Professional Standards for the Accreditation of Schools, Colleges, and Departments of Education." 2001. http://www.ncate.org/standard/m_stds.htm. Accessed Nov. 1, 2002.

National Council of Teachers of English and the International Reading Association. "Standards for the English Language Arts." 2001. http://www.ncte. org/standards/. Accessed Nov. 1, 2002.

National Forum on Information Literacy. "The National Forum on Information Literacy: An Overview." n.d. http://www.infolit.org/. Accessed Nov. 1, 2002.

National Research Council. *Being Fluent with Information Technology*. Washington, D.C.: National Academy Press, 1999, pp. 48–50.

Neuman, Delia. "Designing Databases as Tools for Higher-Level Learning: Insights from Institutional Design." *Educational Technology, Research, and Development*, 1993, *41*, 25–46.

New England Association of Schools and Colleges, Commission on Institutions of Higher Education. "Standard 7: Library and Information Resources, Standards for Accreditation." 2001, p. 19. http://www.neasc.org/cihe/ standards.PDF. Accessed Jan. 3, 2003.

"Newsletter of the California State University Libraries" (Ilene F. Rockman, ed.). *1*(1), 2002. http://www.calstate.edu/LS/A1007.pdf. Accessed Nov. 1, 2002.

Nichols, Janet W. "Building Bridges: High School and University Partnerships for Information Literacy." *NASSP Bulletin*, 1999, *83*(3), 75–81.

Nishimura, Taizo. "Information Literacy: How Does It Differ from Traditional or Computer Literacy?" *TechKnowLogia*, Sept.–Oct. 1999, pp. 13–14. http://www.techknowlogia.org. Accessed Nov. 1, 2001.

Online Computer Library Center. "OCLC White Paper on the Information Habits of College Students." June 2002, pp. 2–3. http://www2.oclc.org/oclc/pdf/printondemand/informationhabits.pdf. Accessed July 1, 2002.

O'Sullivan, Carmel. "Is Information Literacy Relevant in the Real World?" *Reference Services Review*, 2002, *30*(1), 7–14.

Pearson, Debra, and Beth McNeil. "From High School Users College Students Grow: Providing Academic Library Research Opportunities to High School Students." *Knowledge Quest*, 2002, *30*(4), 24–28.

Rader, Hannelore. "User Education and Information Literacy for the Next Decade: An International Perspective." *Reference Services Review*, 1996, *24*(2), 71–75.

Ray, Kathryn, and Joan Day. "Student Attitudes Toward Electronic Resources." *Information Research*, Oct. 1998, *4*(2). http://InformationR.net/ir/4–2/paper54.html. Accessed Nov. 1, 2002.

Rockman, Ilene F. *Library Instruction to EOP Students: A Case Study*. Bethesda, Md.: ERIC Document Reproduction Service, 1978. (ED 174 211)

Roth, Lorie. "Educating the Cut-and-Paste Generation." *Library Journal*, Nov. 1, 1999, *124*(18), 42–44.

Sanford, Stephanie. "Terry Crane: Inspiring Connections." *Converge*, Sept. 2000. http://www.convergemag.com/Publications/CNVGSept00/profilecrane/profile.shtml. Accessed May 3, 2002.

Shapiro, Jeremy J., and Shelley K. Hughes. "Information Literacy as a Liberal Art." *Educom Review*, Mar.–Apr. 1996, *31*(2). http://www.educause.edu/pub/er/review/reviewarticles/31231.html. Accessed Nov. 2, 2002.

Sonntag, Gabriela, Project Director. "High School Project. Information Competence: A Forum Series For High Schools. n.d. http://library.csusm.edu/departments/ilp/ilp_projects/HiSc/ICHS.html

Sonntag, Gabriela, and Donna M. Ohr. "The Development of a Lower-Division, General Education, Course-Integrated Information Literacy Program." *College and Research Libraries*, July 1996, *57*(4), 331–338.

U.S. Department of Labor, The Secretary's Commission on Achieving Necessary Skills. "What Work Requires of Schools: A SCANS Report for America 2000," June 1991. Available from http://www.academicinnovations.com/report.html. Accessed Nov. 1, 2002.

Western Association of Schools and Colleges. "Standard 2." In *Handbook of Accreditation*. Jan. 2001, p. 20. http://www.wascweb.org/senior/handbook.pdf. Accessed Nov. 1, 2002.

Wingspread Group on Higher Education. *An American Imperative: Higher Expectations for Higher Education*. Racine, Wisc.: Johnson Foundation, 1993.

Work Group on Information Competence. "Information Competence in the California State University: A Report." 1995, p. 9. http://www.calstate.edu/LS/Aboutinfocomp.shtml. Accessed Nov. 1, 2002.

1

Developing Faculty-Librarian Partnerships in Information Literacy

Susan Carol Curzon

The cornerstone of an information literacy program that flourishes and endures on a campus is the powerful partnership between faculty and librarians. Faculty have governance of the curriculum, a steady influence on students, and mastery of their discipline. Librarians have exceptional information research skills, knowledge of student searching behavior, and a commitment to the importance of information literacy in the lives of students. Faculty and librarians together can make a formidable team that can sustain an information literacy program that results in information-literate students. The question is "How do we develop a successful partnership between faculty and librarians, and how do we use that partnership to teach information literacy?"

The establishment of a partnership means sharing in an endeavor. The parties must have a mutual interest in the endeavor and see mutual benefit emerging from it. Both parties must give similar weight to the goals and make a similar commitment. However, focusing faculty attention on information literacy, let alone creating an enduring partnership, can present challenges. Faculty have many competing interests. They must teach their classes. They must publish. They must make presentations and attend conferences. They must contribute to the welfare of the university. They must advise students. Most faculty feel that they have established a partnership with librarians, if they have thought about it at all, when they have requested a one-hour BI (bibliographic instruction) session for their students and given class reading lists to the bibliographers. Forming a long-term partnership with librarians to teach information literacy is not at the top of the faculty's agenda.

Fortunately, librarians are not easily deterred. Librarians who are committed to a goal of student mastery of information literacy must establish strategies to create a partnership with faculty. We cannot go it alone. We have to have a partnership with and a base of support from the faculty if we want our students to have information literacy skills.

In this chapter, we will explore the four most important strategies in developing a faculty-librarian partnership that will result in information-literate students. The four strategies are identifying the partners, creating awareness of the issues of information literacy, avoiding partnership pitfalls, and using the partnership to teach information literacy.

Identifying the Partners

Before we embark on a campuswide information literacy program, we have to determine who the partners are that we are targeting. On the surface, it would seem obvious that the partners are simply the faculty; however, faculty play many roles on a campus, and it is important that librarians work with the faculty in each of their roles.

First of all, the academic senate, as the formal representative body of the faculty, will play an important role in the adoption of any goal, such as information literacy, that might affect the curriculum. Information about information literacy must be disseminated to senate members, and a presentation should be made at a senate meeting. Not only the academic senate as a whole but also the individual committees of the senate need to be targeted. Most campuses have an academic senate library committee, an educational policies committee, and an educational resources committee. Librarians should plan on addressing each of these groups to gain support for information literacy. It is also important not to neglect the informal approach, such as meeting with the chair of the academic senate, or with influential faculty in the senate, prior to a senate meeting to explain why information literacy is important to integrate into the curriculum. A meeting with the chair of the senate or with powerful faculty in the senate might help to facilitate achievement of the goals of information literacy.

Another group to target are faculty engaged with centers on teaching and learning. Faculty who are interested in teaching and learning skills often have an appreciation of the need for students to develop core skills such as information literacy. Getting faculty from these centers interested can be very useful for providing support and for getting the word out about the need for information literacy.

Part-time faculty members are another important target audience. Most campuses have a large number of part-time instructors who are often silent members of the faculty. Part-timers teach many of the core courses as well as many courses for freshmen. While part-timers do not direct the curriculum, they are vital to the overall success of any information literacy program because of the number of students that they reach and influence and the nature of the courses that they teach.

Academic administrators are also essential in this partnership. Academic administrators are faculty with the ability to commit budget, space, and personnel resources to an information literacy program; thus, any university-wide goal must have their backing. They will need to be appealed to on two levels—as administrators with resources to deploy and as faculty committed to the welfare of students.

Department chairs are another vital part of a successful information literacy program. As every academic librarian knows, chairs are very powerful on a campus because of their direct link with and influence with the faculty. Many faculty members have limited interest in the life of the campus as a whole but a great deal of interest in the life of their academic department. If a chair supports an information literacy program, it is very likely that many faculty members will be influenced by this support. In addition, the curriculum is first set in the academic departments. Gaining the support of the chair can directly affect the curriculum of a department. If the campus is very large, making it difficult for librarians to meet one-on-one with each chair, librarians should consider attending a chairs' retreat, if available, or the council of chairs, thereby reaching the chairs as a group.

Finally, look for individual professors, full-time or part-time, who may be doing work that would benefit from an information literacy program. Faculty who teach freshman seminars, introductions to the major, service learning courses, developmental English classes, or information research–intensive courses are natural allies to our effort. A few successes with individual professors can be the best public relations for any information literacy effort.

Creating Awareness

The next strategy is to create awareness of the issues of information literacy. In the midst of so much that goes on in the modern university, how can we focus the attention of the faculty on information literacy? No information literacy program can be developed and sustained unless it has a strong base of support. Support can only come when faculty are aware of what information literacy is, why it is important, and what problem it is solving. Librarians have to begin by creating awareness of the issues of information literacy in a way that demonstrates its importance to faculty. Faculty have to understand why it is important to teach and to reinforce the skills of information literacy throughout the academic life of a student. Faculty awareness of information literacy can be raised in the following ways:

First, remember that many faculty will not think of information literacy as requiring much attention. Much of information literacy seems basic to them and so much a part of the fabric of their academic life that they take it for granted. However, faculty are very involved in teaching critical thinking and in producing students who are critical thinkers. Critical thinking is the best platform for a meeting of minds between faculty and librarians. Information literacy supports critical thinking since it emphasizes assessing search results for quality and relevance, and evaluating information choices for reliability, validity, authority, and timeliness before making judgments based upon them. Make a powerful link between critical thinking and information literacy as part of the conversation to interest faculty in the need for student information literacy skills.

Next, talk about information literacy as a lifelong skill. A university educates and civilizes the mind and prepares students to be successful in their life's endeavors. Each generation needs new things. Our students, living in a world of abundant information, need information literacy. It gives students a strategic advantage. Information literacy is particularly important in disciplines, like the sciences or engineering, where the knowledge base can change dramatically every few years. Since faculty want their students to be successful throughout life, they will appreciate that students who graduate with information literacy skills can keep learning throughout life and keep contributing to their profession and to society.

Talk about how information literacy helps students with their current academic endeavors. Learning comprises competencies and content. This means that how we go about learning can be as important as what we learn. For example, we had to learn to read in order to write. We have to learn to be information literate in order to use information effectively. Many faculty can be oblivious as to what happens when students use library resources to write a paper. Faculty certainly see the results, but librarians see the often messy process of students doing information research. The process affects the outcome. If faculty are not happy with the quality of papers and other assignments turned in, they may want to influence the process of information research. This is where the information literacy program comes in.

Remember also to talk about information literacy as one of the essential skills of student academic life. There is literacy, the ability to read and write; mathematical literacy, the ability to understand the fundamentals of mathematics; visual literacy, the ability to understand graphs and charts; media literacy, the ability to critically evaluate information from the media; computer literacy, the ability to use a computer effectively; and information literacy, the ability to find, use, and evaluate information. Students need all of these skills in order to be successful in their academic endeavors.

Finally, faculty do respect data. To create awareness about information literacy, data should be provided about the current level of student information literacy skills. It is one thing to talk about information literacy as an important skill; it is quite another to demonstrate to the faculty the skill level of their own students. They will see the immediate impact and understand the consequences of underskilled students. Without some level of assessment, the conversation will never achieve the importance or the urgency that it should have. One caution here though; showing assessment data to faculty is not without its own problems. Librarians should be prepared to discuss the standards on which the assessment is based and discuss how the test measured those standards. Faculty will want to know how they will know when students are information literate. Carrying out an assessment does open up another arena of partnership. Some librarians might want to involve faculty early by asking their assistance in designing the assessment tools for information literacy.

Of course, creating awareness in the minds of faculty about the need for student mastery of information literacy is not a one-time event. Reports, updates, bulletins, presentations, and many conversations are necessary over an extended period of time to penetrate the collective consciousness of campus faculty and to allow information literacy to rise to the top of the long list of issues confronting campuses today.

Avoiding Partnership Pitfalls

The next strategy is to avoid partnership pitfalls. Not every partnership goes smoothly. Any group of people will have conflicting agendas, different orientations and experiences, and different priorities and interests. Some upset and conflict is inevitable in any partnership, but many problems can be avoided by knowing in advance the most common pitfalls in faculty-librarian partnerships that address the issue of information literacy.

It is imperative that librarians respect faculty authority over the curriculum. Librarians can advise, recommend, and urge but cannot dictate or control the curriculum. Many faculty feel under siege in the university. The curriculum is sometimes the last bastion of their rights. Librarians should be very cautious and avoid awakening the territoriality of the faculty regarding the curriculum.

Most information literacy programs fail because they are parochial and eventually come to be seen as only a library effort. To prevent this, savvy librarians will deploy a strategy that makes the information literacy program part of the educational strategy of the university, not just part of the service program of the library. The information literacy program should be introduced as an enterprise-wide solution to an enterprise-wide problem. To catch the attention of faculty and academic administrators, information literacy must be part of the academic effort rather than just a toolbox of skills that students learn in order to use the library.

Make sure that the information literacy program has goals that are agreed on by the faculty and the librarians. All too often, librarians lay out the goals for information literacy in a canned way to the faculty. But faculty have not spent years reading about information literacy and libraries. They are not so ready to accept the Association of College and Research Libraries standards. They first seek understanding and then, from that understanding, seek to create their own goals. People who share in the creation of goals are more committed to a program than people who have goals delivered to them. Even if it feels to librarians like they are traversing well-traveled roads, it is worth spending time with the faculty to create mutual goals for the program.

Look to use the joint authority of faculty and librarians to develop a program of information literacy. Many librarians claim ownership of the domain of information literacy and are focused on making sure that it remains within library control. Faculty are busy with their own agendas. When they hear a message of exclusiveness, they are only too willing to let it happen elsewhere. The result of a message of exclusiveness is that the librarians will eventually have to go it alone, without the backing and support of the faculty. Instead, librarians should send a message of inclusiveness and should seek every avenue for creating the program with joint faculty-librarian authority.

Librarians should also be mindful of the compactness of the curriculum. Many disciplines are very information-intensive, and many faculty cannot get through all that they want the students to know. If librarians demand too many information literacy sessions, then faculty, feeling under pressure, may simply reject the entire effort. Remember that information literacy supports the curriculum; it does not drive it.

Be careful not to exhaust the faculty by inundating them with a full array of information literacy standards. Occasionally, librarians overprofessionalize information literacy and are too intense about the subject. Instead, ask faculty who are interested in teaching and supporting information literacy to explain to students the process of an information search so that students understand that there is a framework that can be followed. Then ask faculty to work with the students to develop these three essential skills: the ability to articulate the search, the ability to develop a search strategy, and the ability to understand the concept of valid information. More detail can come later, but keeping things simple will keep the faculty engaged, and an engaged faculty means engaged students.

Librarians should also be attentive to the timing of the conversations about information literacy. If there are much higher priorities—for example, budget cuts or a conflict between faculty and administration—this is not the time to launch an information literacy program. First, the discussion will not be heard above the din of the other events, or worse, it might be used as a weapon in the debates on the other issues. When introducing an information literacy program, scan the environment closely and choose the timing wisely.

Despite all that has been written and said about information literacy, be prepared to define it. Most faculty have heard the term but not the definition. Many may have heard the definition but still wonder what it is all about. There are many more who confuse information literacy with computer literacy or information technology. Before any program is started, faculty should be educated about what information literacy is and what it is not. If the faculty do not have a clear definition of information literacy from the start, there will be a lot of confusion and goal misdirection when the information literacy program begins.

Using the Partnership to Teach Information Literacy

Once the partners have been identified, awareness created, and pitfalls avoided, librarians are ready to use the partnership to teach information literacy. If the faculty are convinced of the need for information-literate students and are ready to move forward with solutions, the questions become "How will information literacy be taught? How will students develop a mastery of information literacy?" There are nine models for teaching information literacy that can be used on any campus. One size will not fit all, and each model will have its advantages and disadvantages and will require more or less partnership. Faculty and librarians must consider each model and determine which one or ones best suit the needs of the students and the environment of the campus. Let's explore each of the models.

The Introduction Model

First, there is the introduction model, in which information literacy is incorporated into freshman seminars, orientations, first-year composition courses, and introductions to the major. In this model, information literacy is often being introduced to the students for the first time. The basic concepts are taught, core resources are explored, and assignments that develop information literacy skills are given. This model is particularly fertile ground for faculty-librarian collaboration. The librarian is often a full participant, teaching a module or two in a course or working with faculty on the assignments. The goals of the faculty member and the librarian are closely aligned, and students benefit from this team approach. The downside of this model is that curriculum committees often view the use of the introduction model as completing the teaching of information literacy. As any librarian knows, one or two class hours on information literacy are not enough to allow students to grasp this skill. Regardless, the introduction model should be widely used because it reaches the widest number of students.

General Education Model

The second is the general education (GE) model, in which information literacy is incorporated into GE goals and also into certification and recertification of GE courses. In this model, as in the introduction model, librarians and faculty must work closely, because information literacy instruction is spread throughout many courses. Librarians must help articulate the goals of information literacy and develop the grids for the information literacy certification of courses. They also must be prepared to deliver on the demand that will be created by that many courses with an information literacy component. Faculty must support and vote for inclusion of information literacy in the GE requirements and then be prepared to develop and commit to some assignments with an information literacy emphasis. True partnership comes because faculty and librarians have a shared responsibility in advancing information literacy. The downside of this model is that the goals of information literacy can become dispersed and drift as information literacy instruction is spread out across the university unless a core group of people remains willing to champion the cause. In addition, sometimes information literacy gets caught in the cross fire of competing GE requirements in either the lower division or the upper division.

The Learning Outcomes Model

The third model is the learning outcomes model, in which the academic departments write information literacy into the learning outcome goals of their department. The great advantage of this model is that there is strong commitment from faculty when information literacy is centered in and motivated from the departments. Also, most academic departments assess their learning outcomes, and when something is assessed, it tends to occur. However, this model can suffer from the same disadvantage as the GE model in that information literacy instruction may become so widely dispersed that it is difficult to ascertain fully what is occurring and to what level of attainment. This model also calls for strong faculty-librarian partnership, because librarians often must work with each department to develop the learning outcomes and then be prepared to deal with the increased demand for information literacy sessions.

Information Literacy Course Model

Many librarians yearn for their campus to have a course on information literacy, preferably required of all incoming students. Librarians see a course as one of the best ways to make sure that students have the information literacy skills that they need. An entire semester's focus on information literacy gives students a thorough grounding that, it is hoped, will last throughout their lives. On the surface, it might appear that there is not much need for faculty-librarian partnership in this model. But no librarian can get a course on information literacy offered without the approval of faculty curriculum committees. Faculty must see the value of the course and be willing to support it. Librarians who want the support of faculty for a course should be prepared to have discussions with faculty on whether information literacy can stand alone as a skill or whether it must be attached to a discipline. There is no right answer, because both are correct. There are basic concepts that can be taught separately from a discipline, but it is also true that information literacy skill development is enriched when it is attached to a discipline.

Librarians also need to make sure that the resources to offer the class will be coming their way. The support of the provost is essential, since a library is not in the usual budget formula for courses. Librarians pursuing a course that is required should also keep in mind that requiring a new course means that another course somewhere else must be deleted; only so many units can be sustained in the GE or major program. This can engender a difficult and prolonged debate. Faculty must be very committed to a goal in order to surrender resources for a course on information literacy.

Demonstration of Mastery Model

The fifth model is the demonstration of mastery model, in which students demonstrate their mastery of information literacy by taking a test.

This model is usually linked with a graduation or GE requirement in order to make sure that students actually take the test. Often, to avoid battles over credit, this test is made a requirement without units. This model has certain advantages. Once the test is developed, students can take it on-line, receive quick feedback, and retake it if needed. Also, this model is not as resource-intensive as the other models; for example, it does not require significant personnel. Another advantage is that it is one of the few models that reaches all of the students. One disadvantage is that aside from the initial creation of the test and occasional changes, there is minimal faculty-librarian partnership. While an assessment of the student pass rate can be regularly provided to faculty, they will still think that information literacy instruction is something that happens elsewhere. As a result of this minimal interaction, it is not likely that the skill level of students in information literacy will be very advanced. Students will just view the information literacy test as one more thing to do to meet graduation requirements. Information literacy may not come as alive for them as it would in a course. For all of these reasons, this model is best used in conjunction with other models.

Faculty Focus Model

Some librarians elect not to be involved in direct teaching but instead to put their effort toward increasing support for faculty to teach information literacy in their courses. This requires substantial partnership, because the librarians need to skillfully assess what tools faculty need and then develop them. It is important to caution that this model must not be seen as training the faculty; that interpretation will be resented and rejected. Instead, librarians should think of this model as providing tools to support faculty in their classroom teaching. Tools that librarians might help develop range from guidelines for effective information research assignments to on-line information literacy tutorials that can be integrated with classroom assignments to workshops that feature faculty successes with information literacy assignments. The advantage of this model is that information literacy can be woven into many courses, which means that many students can be reached. In addition, information literacy is being taught by professors, which means that there is more impact on the students, partly because it is linked to grades. The downside of this model is that it is a hit-or-miss approach. Some faculty will be interested; some will not. Thus, this model is best used in conjunction with other models.

The College Readiness Model

The seventh model is the college readiness model. Increasingly, we see entering students who are inadequately prepared, lacking the core skills needed to succeed in college life. In this model, we reach out to the high schools to help them increase the information literacy skills of their students. College librarians partner with school librarians, school faculty, and college faculty who are also interested in increasing the readiness of high school students for college. The disadvantage of this model is that it can be quite difficult. High schools have many requirements and restrictions, and there are usually a number of high school districts that feed into a college, meaning that work has to be done across multiple jurisdictions and bureaucracies. Working out a sustained program with any high school requires determination and a long-term commitment. The advantage, of course, is that students are much better prepared when they enter college.

Librarians should consider targeting faculty in colleges of education for a program on information literacy. These faculty are teaching the future teachers. If librarians want to really influence a generation, it is important to get to the K–12 teachers, so that they understand the issues of information literacy and think that teaching information literacy is valuable. The best time to reach K–12 teachers is while they are still in college and learning the art and practice of teaching. Reaching their professors can be very worthwhile in terms of affecting the college readiness of students.

The Entrance Requirement Model

The entrance requirement model means that high school students would be required to take an information literacy test before entering college. This model has the advantage of sending a clear message that information literacy is to be taken seriously by those who plan the curriculum in high schools. Many high school librarians would welcome such a message from a university, which would lend support to their own program. This would also be true of community college librarians whose students are transferring to a four-year university. This model is not without its challenges, though. First, librarians would need to partner with faculty from the university and the high school to get agreement on the idea of implementing a test and on the content of the test. The tough debate here for faculty and librarians would center on what level of information literacy skills entering students are expected to have. There also has to be agreement on what to do if students fail the test. No failure on an information literacy test is going to prevent students from going to college. Therefore, librarians and faculty would have to be ready to provide remedial or development sessions to get the students to the needed skill level. To a great extent, offering a remedial program is what many librarians are doing now.

The On-Demand Model

The ninth and last model is the on-demand model, which is the prevailing model in most libraries today. In this model, a faculty member contacts the librarian, asks for an information research session on the on-line catalogue and the most important electronic journals and a tour of the library. If the librarian is lucky, he or she can squeeze in the basic concepts of information literacy. The advantage of this model is the continual dialogue between the faculty and the librarians about course needs. It is also advantageous because information literacy is incorporated into classroom teaching and so is very relevant to students' immediate academic needs. The downside of the model is that information literacy instruction is often only an hour or two. This model is also a hit-or-miss strategy, with the result that some students go through their entire educational career without the important ingredient of information literacy training.

No one model is perfect. Each has its advantages and disadvantages, and each requires different levels of partnership between faculty and librarians. A combination of models that reaches every student at different points in his or her academic career is ideal. One recommendation is the following combination: the introduction model, because it reaches all freshmen and transfer students; the learning outcomes model, because information competence is incorporated into the curriculum; the faculty focus model, because it encourages the teaching of information literacy in the classroom; the on-demand model, because information literacy instruction is tailored to students' immediate needs; and the entrance requirement model, because it ensures that students will arrive with a high level of information literacy. No matter what model or models are deployed, the key ingredient is the ability of the faculty and the librarians to use their partnership to teach information literacy.

Conclusion

Here is the bottom line: if students are not information literate, they cannot use information effectively. If students cannot use information effectively, they cannot function effectively in their studies. Regardless of the model or models that are chosen to teach information literacy, librarians and faculty must partner to teach students information literacy skills. With information literacy skills, a student's academic life is deeply enriched, their academic achievement enabled, and their capacity for lifelong learning is enhanced. When our students have mastery over information literacy, librarians and faculty have done their job as educators. Information literacy is an important cause. All the preservation, organization, and dissemination of information goes to waste if students are unable to use information effectively. The challenge before librarians and faculty is to teach information literacy so that it enables students to succeed in their education, to have a core skill that will give them a strategic advantage, and to build a lifelong skill that will make their lives richer with an educated understanding and use of information.

Further Reading

Breivik, Patricia Senn. "Information Literacy and the Engaged Campus." *AAHE Bulletin*, Nov. 2000, 53(3), 3–6.

Germain, Carol Anne, Trudi E. Jacobsen, and Sue A. Kazcor. "A Comparison of the Effectiveness of Presentation Formats for Instruction: Teaching First Year Students." *College and Research Libraries News*, Jan. 2000, *61*, 65–72.

Intersegmental Committee of the Academic Senates of the California Community Colleges, the California State University, and the University of California. *Academic Literacy: A Statement of Competencies Expected of Students Entering California's Public Colleges and Universities*. Sacramento. Intersegmental Committee of the Academic Senates of the California Community Colleges, the California State University, and the University of California, Spring 2002. Also available at http://www.academicsenate. cc.ca.us/publications/papers/academicliteracy/main.htm.

Leckie, Gloria J., and Anne Fullerton. "Information Literacy in Science and Engineering Undergraduate Education: Faculty Attitudes and Pedagogical Practices." *College and Research Libraries*, Jan. 1999, 60(1), 9–29.

Online Computer Library Center. "How Academic Librarians Can Influence Students' Web-Based Information Choices." In "OCLC White Paper on the Information Habits of College Students." June 2002. http://www2.oclc.org/oclc/pdf/printondemand/informationhabits.pdf.

Raspa, Dick, and Dane Ward. *The Collaborative Imperative: Librarians and Faculty Working Together in the Information Universe*. Chicago: Association of College and Research Libraries, 2000.

Rockman, Ilene. "More Than Faculty Training: Integrating Information Competence into the Disciplines." *College and Research Libraries* Mar. 2000, 61(3), 192–194.

Roth, Lorie. "Educating the Cut-and-Paste Generation." *Library Journal*, Nov. 1, 1999, 124(18), 42–44

Rury, John L. "Inquiry in the General Education Curriculum." *JGE: The Journal of General Education*, 1996, 45(3), 175–196.

"21st Century Literacy." ALA Action No. 1. Chicago: American Library Association, 2001.

Young, Rosemary M., and Stephen Harmony. *Working with Faculty to Design Undergraduate Information Literacy Programs*. New York: Neal-Schuman, 1999.

2

Successful Strategies for Integrating Information Literacy into the Curriculum

Ilene F. Rockman

Integrating information literacy into the curriculum can take many forms. Successful models can result from collaborations with various campus units such as teacher education programs, freshman seminars and first-year experience programs, residential learning communities, writing across the curriculum programs, faculty development centers, service learning units, and information technology programs that support on-line and distance education classes. These efforts can result in heightened interest in and awareness of the importance of information literacy.

Teacher Education

As state governments continue to re-evaluate their preparation and support programs for new teachers, opportunities exist to include information literacy competencies in the curriculum delivered to pre-service teachers. The quality of preparation for new teachers entering the classroom can be enhanced by coursework and student teaching experiences that prepare them to address any information need. In addition, they need the skills to teach their students, in turn, how to dissect the complexities of finding, evaluating, using, and communicating information. It is no surprise that politicians and lay citizens are desirous of a well-qualified teaching force that keeps current with course content, instructional strategies, and student learning styles.

In 1994, Pete Wilson, the governor of California, signed legislation that directed the California Commission on Teacher Credentialing to assess the extent to which teacher education programs in the state prepared elementary and secondary teacher candidates in critical thinking and problem-solving skills (Paul, Elder, and Bartell, 2002). Researchers conducted 140 interviews and found that although the overwhelming majority (89 percent) of education faculty and faculty in academic disciplines indicated that critical thinking was a primary objective of their instruction, based on their answers, only 9 percent were teaching for critical thinking on a typical day. It is clear that more needs to be done to help these faculty members integrate information literacy and critical thinking into their instruction. If adults do not possess these important information literacy "survival" skills, they will not be able to effectively teach their students to become proficient, ethical users and producers of information in a multicultural, globally connected world. Carr (1998) notes, "If teachers are to use information so that others can learn from them, then teachers must be information literate."

One way to assist teachers is to model practical, useful lesson plans that can be adapted to any classroom setting. At all costs, what is to be avoided is the lament "I wish someone had taught me this earlier" (Asselin and Lee, 2002).

A method that has proven successful in advancing information literacy in teacher education programs is problem-based learning, which fosters active, self-directed learning; develops critical thinking skills; and integrates content with technology. It is an instructional strategy that takes real-life, everyday situations and creates learning opportunities from them (Macklin, 2001). Problem-based learning engages and motivates learners because the topics are open-ended, complex problems with no predetermined solutions, are often interdisciplinary in nature, and build on student interests. Within this environment, students are given opportunities for reflection and assessment, in order to develop the critical thinking skills that lead to information literacy and ultimately to transfer their learning to other situations. Cooperative work groups help learners to communicate with each other, critically analyze and solve problems, base decisions on facts (after finding, synthesizing, and evaluating information sources), and develop lifelong learning skills. At the conclusion of the problem-based learning experience, students demonstrate their newly acquired knowledge.

When teacher candidates have had a chance to engage in problem-based learning opportunities that incorporate information literacy principles, it is easier for them to incorporate these principles into the development of lesson plans and learning opportunities for their own students. It is essential for them to have these learning experiences as pre-service teachers so that they will have the maximum opportunity to successfully pass along these experiences and transfer this knowledge to students within their own classrooms.

Rader (1997, p. 49) notes, "Teachers must develop instructional skills to provide an interactive classroom learning climate where students can solve problems and learn cooperatively." The following resources can help in this effort.

> *Teaching Information Retrieval and Evaluation Skills for Education Students and Practitioners: A Casebook of Applications*, edited by Patricia O'Brien Libutti and Bonnie Gratch (1995), is a useful toolkit that provides scenarios, cases, lessons, and instructional materials to encourage interactions between teachers and students.
>
> *Information Power: Building Partnerships for Learning*, published by the American Association of School Librarians (1998), contains nine standards for student learning focused on information literacy, independent learning, and social responsibility.

The Big6, developed by Michael B. Eisenberg and Robert E. Berkowitz, is a widely used problem-solving approach to teaching information and technology skills. On the Web site (http://www.big6.com), teachers can find sample information literacy lesson plans and links to resources, research studies, and assessment tools.

Teacher Researchers at Work, by Marion S. McLean and Marion M. Mohr (1999), describes a method in which teachers engage in reflective practice and ask questions about what they observe in the classroom, using student work as data to improve their teaching and their students' learning.

Templeton and Warner (2002, p. 71) stress the importance of incorporating information literacy into teacher education programs, using the newly revised standards from the National Council for the Accreditation of Teacher Education (NCATE), which state that those preparing to work in schools must be able to "appropriately and effectively integrate technology and information literacy in instruction to support student learning."

Unless teacher education candidates are exposed to the principles of information literacy as part of their professional educational experiences, it is unlikely that they will learn how to effectively find, use, and evaluate information. Worse, they will be unable to teach these important concepts to their students, the next generation of learners, who must learn to flourish in an information-rich environment.

Freshman Seminars and First-Year Experience Programs

A generation ago, the notion of a freshman seminar or first-year college experience program was not well known. Today, under the leadership of the Policy Center on the First Year of College at Brevard College in North Carolina, the concept is becoming more commonplace on college and university campuses of all sizes and in all locations. Institutions have realized that it is in their interest to engage students in the learning process early in their academic career, in order to improve retention and establish a positive, nurturing relationship with their future alumni.

In April 2002, the center conducted its fifth national survey of first-year programs in American higher education and reported that of 1,013 institutions surveyed, 749 (73.9 percent) offered a special course for first-year students, such as a first-year seminar, colloquium, or student success course.

These courses are becoming more important as we read about the remedial needs of freshman students entering higher education. Recent reports show that just 41 percent of the 37,870 incoming freshmen in the California State University system in fall 2002 demonstrated the ability to perform college-level math and English (St. John, 2003). Although the system's chief academic officer attributes the problem to students' lack of ability to read critically, comprehend what they read, and overcome difficulties with English as a second language, educators know that a solution to these problems is complex and deeply rooted, requiring time and resources to rectify.

To help alleviate the problems that freshmen have in adjusting to the rigors of college life, many undergraduate libraries have reached out to secondary schools to help prepare students for the academic transition to the college and university setting as well as become actively involved with freshman seminar and first-year learning programs on their campuses. These programs are often linked with other college or university programs (such as learning communities) and are intended to help students successfully meet the academic standards of college as well as receive the academic and emotional support they need to "survive" during their initial campus year.

Boff and Johnson (2002) suggest that first-year experience (FYE) courses are excellent venues for introducing freshman students to information literacy concepts. According to their national survey, a majority of FYE programs contain some type of library or research component, although many programs limit the time devoted to information literacy instruction by focusing, instead, on such subjects as an orientation to the university environment, test taking skills, time management strategies, setting personal goals, developing moral character, learning how to be a successful citizen in a globally connected multicultural world, being a socially responsible citizen on campus, and recommendations for exploring career options. A generation ago such courses or seminars were not part of the university experience, but now these courses are prominent components of the higher education curriculum.

At Bowling Green State University in Ohio, the library is actively involved with the first-year experience program on campus. A first-year experience librarian works cooperatively with instructors to help reduce student anxiety about researching a paper by providing library instructional sessions and creating library modules, exercises, and tutorials that can be integrated into courses targeted specifically for first-year students (http://www.bgsu.edu/colleges/library/infoserv/libraryfyi/).

The freshman interest groups (FIGs) at the University of Washington are well known as a successful program for students, peer advisers, and faculty members. Incoming freshmen take a cluster of courses together, meet periodically with an upper-class peer adviser, and have ample opportunities to share knowledge, establish friendships, gain social support, and learn about university resources. In 1994, technology and information literacy were incorporated in FIGs via the UWired program. Meeting in the UWired laptop collaboratory, students learn about electronic communication, information navigation, and information evaluation. Special groups, such as campus athletes, are also included in the UWired program (Pierard and Graves, 2002, p. 80). The library continues to play an active role in the program, and in 1998 it offered a two-credit information literacy course not only to help students become fluent with information technology (e-mail, word processing, and presentation software) but also to enhance their research skills (using subscription databases and the World Wide Web, evaluating information sources, citing print and electronic sources properly) and writing skills.

At Northern Kentucky University, library faculty are actively involved with the University 101 course for freshmen, shaping group-based assignments to maximize collaborative learning opportunities, creating and delivering workshops for course instructors to inform them about library services and resources, and by promoting contact between students, instructors, and the library. Results have led to a decrease in student library anxiety and a change in freshman perceptions to seeing the library research process as one requiring "forethought, flexibility, reasoning, judgment, and analysis" (Werrell, 1997, p. 176).

At George Mason University, faculty and librarians work together to integrate information literacy into a yearlong first-year learning community program with a common curriculum. The collaboration is based on mutual respect, and the librarian is closely involved in curriculum design (Young and Williams, 2003, p. 19).

The approach taken by California State University, Chico, in its three-credit first-year experience course is that half of the curriculum should focus on information and computer competencies (Blakeslee, Owens, and Dixon, 2001). The instructors note that the ability to use information technology is an everyday part of today's university and that the majority of first-year students lack the requisite skills to be comfortable and successful in a technological environment; thus, the course will devote 50 percent of its time to helping students develop these competencies. The instructors want their students to be able to easily and successfully check a course schedule on the university's World Wide Web site; communicate with a professor about an assignment using e-mail technology; and find, evaluate, and use information to write a research paper.

At Marysville College in Tennessee, the first-year curriculum includes information literacy skills that directly support the educational

goals of the college: (1) critical thinking, inquiry, and decision making and (2) the ability to retrieve and synthesize information and
to complete independent research (Nugent and Myers, 2000). Students use these skills as they complete the first-year requirements of
the January Freshman Seminar, and the Spring Freshman Research
Seminar.

And at the University of the Pacific, information literacy skills
are incorporated into a general education program for college freshmen in which students participate in a mentor seminar program
lasting two semesters (Fenske and Clark, 1995).

All of these institutions recognize the importance of weaving
information literacy into the lower-division curriculum. As Tsui
notes, "Students deserve challenging coursework from the start of
their freshmen year" (2001, p. 20). Information literacy has a clear
and strong contribution to make toward meeting this goal. Academic librarians can play a significant role in the first-year experience
program by becoming actively involved in curriculum development
for courses such as freshman seminars, teaching sections of first-year
experience courses, offering information literacy courses linked to
the first-year experience program, and promoting the development
of information literacy skills that students can transfer from course
to course throughout their academic and post-university careers.
Such involvement by librarians early in a student's university experience is essential in order to break down barriers to learning and
increase student comfort levels with managing information so that
they can successfully complete course requirements and attain the
skills needed for self-directed lifelong learning.

Residential Learning Communities

Co-curricular learning is important for a well-rounded student experience. Co-curricular programs include residential learning communities, which integrate academic learning, academic assistance,

and community living. The Residential Learning Community International Registry lists more than one hundred institutions that have such programs.

On the Web page for the University of Michigan's living/learning communities (http//www.lib.umich.edu/ugl/services/llc/), one can read that the program offers the "benefits of a small liberal arts college with the resources of a large university." One of these resources is the university library's print and digital collections, and another is the excellent staff of university librarians to help faculty incorporate library assignments into course requirements and to help students understand the research process through effective evaluation of information resources such as Web pages, books, government publications, and journal articles.

At Sonoma State University, information competence is seamlessly integrated into students' first-year experiences. The Educational Mentoring Team Program, an advising and orientation program offered to all first-time freshmen, includes the freshman seminar, a one-semester course taught by a team of instructors, including a librarian. The freshman interest group program offers freshmen the opportunity to participate in a living/learning community, in which they develop information literacy skills in a supportive environment (http://libweb.sonoma.edu/brodsky/infocomp/training.html).

Within the last few years, librarians on many campuses have become more actively involved in residential learning communities by helping to ensure that all facilities are connected to the campus network; providing students with evening and weekend workshops on the fundamentals of information literacy; and training residential advisers, who, in turn, can provide preliminary help to students. Librarians also promote virtual reference services that offer real-time reference and instructional assistance through the Internet.

In addition, librarians are sharing their expertise with others at professional meetings such as the Conference on Living-Learning

Programs and Residential Colleges (http://www.osuhousing.com/conference/). At the 2001 meeting of this conference, L. Marc Goldman from the University of Illinois at Urbana-Champaign presented a paper titled "Learning Organizations in the Face of Living-Learning: Library Professionals as One Catalyst." On his campus, the university's Residential Hall Library System (RHLS) includes eight libraries that are maintained, managed, and operated by the Housing Division, working collaboratively with the university's undergraduate library. Their goals are to provide academic support for students living in the residence halls, help students to become confident information seekers and lifelong learners, provide collections to support the needs of first- and second-year students, and offer personal and tailored library instructional sessions.

The university libraries at the University of Maryland are also actively involved with all living/learning programs on campus. An undergraduate studies librarian provides outreach services that connect librarians with students and faculty involved in the living/learning programs. Such services include helping faculty to link information literacy instruction to themes and courses, and providing reference and research assistance on site in the residence halls where the living/learning programs take place.

It is clear that libraries have an important role to play in the development, enhancement, and expansion of residential learning communities. With increased librarian outreach efforts, their services are now more accessible to students, helping them in a non-threatening way to become confident, independent learners through formal and informal information literacy learning opportunities.

Writing Across the Curriculum Programs

On many campuses, writing across the curriculum refers to a university-wide program that focuses on teaching writing within the context of academic disciplines. Writing across the curriculum engages learning within subject content. Information literacy programs can emulate this integrative model. Information literacy instruction can be infused within academic departments, strengthening students' research skills.

Elmborg (2003, p. 68) suggests that information literacy librarians can learn from the experiences of writing across the curriculum programs. Integrating information competencies into the learning outcomes of academic disciplines shifts the responsibility for information literacy instruction from the library to the entire campus community. Such a shift in thinking and action requires faculty to take responsibility for both teaching and assessing these important skills within their departmental courses and capstone experiences.

Just as writing shapes and enhances thought, clarifies thinking, and facilitates learning, so does information literacy. Both are interdisciplinary, employ technology, and contribute to lifelong learning.

Writing across the curriculum and writing in the discipline programs show no signs of abating, since evidence of successful program implementation continues to increase (Sensenbaugh, 1993). These programs span both the lower division and the upper division. Sheridan (1995) has written a thoughtful guide showing the connections between critical thinking, the research process, and the composition process. Such linkages are natural, because it is clear that developing their research skills will also improve students' writing skills. Assignments as simple as keeping a personal research log or a journal support information literacy skills by developing the complementary skills of reflective thinking, analysis, decision making, problem solving, and writing. A log or journal is the researcher's written account of the progress of the research process, in which he or she answers such questions as "What did I do?" "What did I find?" "What did I learn?" "How did I feel?" In this way, the journal becomes a tool for evaluating the information, the search process, and the learning that took place (California School Library Association, 1997).

Gibson (1995, p. 57) has written about the connections between writing skills and research skills. He notes that student writers and student researchers share the activities of inquiry and investigation. Being an information problem solver can be viewed as similar to being a mature writer; both must think creatively, critically, and strategically to accomplish goals.

Bean (1996, p. 201) writes about why students plagiarize: "Good research writing is intellectually demanding and cognitively complex," which causes students to plagiarize because "they have no other coping mechanism" when assignments seem beyond their capacities. Bean suggests that the teaching of research writing can be strengthened by such strategies as requiring a prospectus of preliminary research well in advance of the final due date. Such a prospectus can ask students to address why their research question is important, how far along they are in their thinking and what they expect to discover, and what sources they have already found (through submission of an annotated working bibliography).

As students enter the higher education environment from various preparatory backgrounds, it is also important to be clear about performance expectations. The Intersegmental Committee of the Academic Senates of the California Community Colleges, the California State University, and the University of California, in the document *Academic Literacy: A Statement of Competencies Expected of Students Entering California's Public Colleges and Universities*, notes, "While many entering students are familiar with some technological elements (notably e-mail and Web browsing), few demonstrate the critical ability to evaluate online resources. Students need to form questioning habits when they are reading, and this is especially true of the material found on the Internet" (2002, p. 33). Together, writing instructors and information literacy librarians can help students to develop these important lifelong learning skills.

Faculty Development Centers

At colleges and universities across the country, faculty development centers are often housed within the university library. This close relationship is advantageous for several reasons: to help faculty reshape their courses in an electronic environment, to incorporate technology (including online catalogs, subject-specific databases, and full-text electronic resources) into their assignments, and to encourage them to integrate information literacy principles into the learning outcomes of their courses. Since information literacy is common to all disciplines, all learning environments, and all levels of higher education, it is desirable for the library to establish a close working relationship with the campus faculty development center (Iannuzzi, 1998).

Some centers have been able to provide support through a teaching fellows program in which selected faculty members offer several hours per week of uninterrupted support to fellow faculty members. On some campuses, the faculty development positions are filled by librarians who have expertise in distance education, Web-based learning, and information literacy. Fellows may do tasks such as the following:

- Help teachers integrate information literacy skills into course management and learning programs such as Blackboard and WebCT

- Help teachers assess student retention of information literacy skills through electronic portfolios and other means

- Help teachers move their courses into an on-line or hybrid learning environment

- Suggest ways to incorporate electronic learning materials (e-books, e-course reserve readings, full-text electronic journal articles) into courses

- Provide guidance and inspiration to teachers about teaching in smart classrooms—classrooms equipped with a network connection, computer, microphone, and projection system so that faculty can teach with data and video technology, engage students, display electronic lessons, and model effective search practices.

- Guide teachers through the process of understanding software tools for preventing Web-based plagiarism

At Florida International University, the library and the Academy for the Art of Teaching work closely together on a model of information literacy that integrates teaching, reflective thinking, and student learning. Information literacy is the doorway to the disciplines that will help students develop their critical thinking skills. Director Leora Baron notes, "Faculty members quickly discover that becoming information literate has its rewards in increasing their abilities to provide students with new and refined tools for academic success and in expanding their own ability to refine and expand research activities" (Baron, n.d.).

At California State University, Hayward, the Faculty Center for Excellence in Teaching has sponsored several programs in conjunction with the university library. These programs included a workshop on plagiarism (why students plagiarize, teaching strategies to minimize this behavior, university policies to address incidents of plagiarism, and software detection programs); a workshop on the pedagogy of information competence; and a weeklong summer workshop to help faculty members reconceptualize their class assignments in order to incorporate information literacy principles (Rockman, 2000).

As places for communication and collaboration, faculty development centers and university libraries have much in common. Together, they can promote and advance information literacy on the campus, reach out to new and seasoned faculty members, and make a difference in the lives of students through collective emphasis on vital tools for lifelong learning.

Service Learning

Service learning is a type of experiential learning that connects real-life work experiences with the college or university curriculum. Students have opportunities to improve academic learning through field experiences in community agencies, nonprofit offices, or other settings. These field experiences serve community needs, help foster civic education (Riddle, 2003, p. 71), and are an integral part of students' coursework. Integrating information literacy principles into service learning programs can have a mutually beneficial outcome to students as they learn to develop and use research skills within the real world of their communities. Examples include being able to provide clients in a clinic or agency with the most up-to-date and accurate information in order to solve a problem.

At Southwest Missouri State University, undergraduates learn about research strategies and information resources in Library and Information Science 101, then team up with clients from community service agencies who need information or who need training to locate and evaluate information. Through this process, students are able to see and feel the power of information while strengthening their self-confidence, communication skills, and ability to find, evaluate, and use information efficiently and effectively. Reflective activities enable them to better understand why developing information literacy skills is important.

At Lehigh University in Pennsylvania, teams of students participate in community-oriented research projects focused on regional economic development. Students participate in the design and execution of specific research projects identified by the Lehigh Valley development agency, such as transportation barriers to successful welfare-to-work transitions. For example, students researched and documented the extent to which women living in the inner city of Allentown were limited in their employment searches by bus route configurations. Students met with regional planners to discuss modifications to the transportation routes or to suggest other ways to promote successful transitions from welfare to work. Throughout the process, students enhanced not only their research skills but also their skills in critical thinking, time management, decision making, civic responsibility, community engagement, problem solving, and oral and written communication.

California State University, Monterey Bay, an outcomes-based campus, requires all undergraduate students to take two courses that integrate classroom learning with service in a community agency or school where they will work with people of different cultures. Since 1995, students have provided over 100,000 hours of meaningful service to over 385 organizations in the area. At the freshman level, students also take a class that helps them become proficient in computer and information literacy. These combined experiences of service learning and information literacy help students to understand how they are connected to the world around them and how having information retrieval and evaluation skills helps them perform better in those real-life situations whether they are helping parents in a day care center to find information about good parenting skills or searching for current health care information when working in a wellness clinic.

Because of the importance of information literacy and service learning, the Historically Black Colleges and Universities Faculty Development Network has focused on this topic for its Third Annual Summer Institute in 2004. Titled "Transforming the Curriculum Through Innovations in Technology, Information Literacy and Service Learning" (http://hbcufdn.org/Sum_Inst.pdf), the institute will take place at Norfolk State University in Virginia.

Berea College in Kentucky has had a long tradition of service learning for many years. Its Center for Excellence in Learning Through Service is a nucleus of support for and information about service learning on campus. The center's Web page provides links to such service learning courses as "Entrepreneurship for the Public Good" and "Service, Citizenship, and Community." Students enrolled in these courses gain opportunities to put their information literacy abilities into practice while developing their skills in civic responsibility, teamwork, leadership, and communication. In a sophomore-level health class, students work on a variety of regional community health projects in coordination with the county health department. Students use their information literacy skills to search for and evaluate information to use in designing an information Web site or in preparing community education programs for the citizens of Appalachia (http://www.berea.edu/cclts/vol2iss2.pdf).

Clearly, information literacy skills have much to offer in enhancing a student's service learning experiences. Jacoby (2003, p. 323), writing about service learning partnerships for the future, notes that a "seamless web that is fundamental to developing the potential of young people and enabling each to become a full participant in our democracy is that of information literacy." When faculty creativity, student ingenuity, and librarian savvy are blended together, powerful and sustained learning results.

On-line and Distance Education Programs

Libraries have an important role to play in helping faculty members who are creating and teaching courses in a Web-based, distance learning, or on-line environment. Librarians can recommend how best to advance information literacy principles in an electronic environment. For example, they can

- Identify resources to support the learning objectives of a course, such as full-text journal articles, government documents, e-books, and quality Internet resources

- Consult on the design and creation of assignments so that students have maximum opportunities to succeed

- Develop instructional support materials such as electronic pathfinders, guides to the literature, webliographies, research tools, Web-based research exercises, and self-paced, interactive tutorials to help students gain skills in search strategy development, critical thinking, and information evaluation

- Suggest links to an around-the-clock electronic mail or virtual reference service to assist learners on demand

- Facilitate remote access to databases within course management systems

- Help to create course-based, customizable library Web pages

- Provide convenient methods of document delivery for information not available in electronic formats

- Set up e-alerts so that users can receive journal tables of contents on a regular basis and keep current in their field even when they are away from the traditional library

Students enrolled in distance learning or on-line courses should have services that mirror those provided to students enrolled in regular "on ground" courses. Whether remote students receive their courses through satellite or cable television transmission, interactive videoconferencing that provides face-to-face interaction between teachers and students, Web-based software, traditional videotapes, or print materials, information literacy instruction is an essential component of the teaching and learning process. Students enrolled in individual courses or degree programs need access to quality information resources provided by the library, but they also need guidance on how to effectively find, analyze, evaluate, and ethically use these resources.

Universities are recognizing that distance education students are all *students*—part-time or full-time, working or not working, single or with families, young or old. It is also not uncommon for students to take one or two classes on campus, along with an on-line course.

A pilot study conducted by the University of Michigan's science librarians in conjunction with a Writing for Biology class indicated that remote, real-time library instruction via cable television could have a positive impact on student learning (Zilius and Tenofsky, 2000). In this vein, librarians at Plattsburgh State University in upstate New York (part of the State University of New York system) provide a wide range of instructional services for interactive video and Internet courses through librarian site visits, a credit-bearing library research distance learning course, Internet research guides, and in-class demonstrations (Jacobson and Williams, 2000, p. 193).

Master's and doctoral students at Nova Southeastern University (NSU) in Florida benefit from librarian assistance in developing information literacy skills and abilities. Librarians prepare on-line research guides, work with faculty to integrate information literacy principles into course syllabi, and offer instructional sessions to meet the needs of these adult learners. NSU was chartered in 1964 and established as its primary goal "the delivery of education to adult students, especially working professionals who could not give up their jobs to attend school full time. This goal automatically led Nova to become a pioneer in the field of distance education" (http://www.undergrad.nova.edu/online/history.cfm).

Distance and on-line education students at California State University, Chico, benefit from the collaboration between professors and librarians to receive both information literacy instruction and live chat reference assistance wherever they are located, whenever they need it. Using special software, librarians offer real-time, interactive reference assistance to users over the Internet. Using HorizonLive, a virtual classroom product, librarians are able to use streaming media (real-time audio and video transmissions), chat, shared applications, PowerPoint slides, and other Web-based technologies to reach and instruct users (Blakeslee and Johnson, 2002).

With technology changing so rapidly, resulting in the development of new tools for teaching and learning,, librarians have found it useful to employ such interactive discussion tools as instant messaging to handle one-on-one instructional queries, Internet Relay Chat (and other software) for reference consultations with more than one person at a time, and Web boards for chat and threaded discussions with students. Bernie Sloan (http://alexia.lis.uiuc.edu/~b-sloan/bernie.htm) at the University of Illinois at Urbana-Champaign maintains numerous lists, bibliographies, papers, and reports about collaborative digital reference and technology-enriched instructional services.

According to the "ACRL Guidelines for Distance Learning Library Services" (1998), "access to adequate library services and resources is essential for the attainment of superior academic skills in post-secondary education." Most notably, the guidelines explicitly emphasize the importance of lifelong learning, which can best be attained through information literacy instruction.

Conclusion

In this globally connected world, with its growing population and vast amounts of information, the ability to continually learn, to be able to find and evaluate useful information, to think critically, and to solve problems is of increasing importance. Information literacy is the key, and one need only look around the world to see that information literacy skills are being discussed, taught, and incorporated into curricula from Atlanta to Zimbabwe.

Information literacy is truly a new instructional pedagogy and a change agent for learning. Only by working with educational stakeholders on and off the campus can information literacy goals be achieved. Partnering with teacher education programs, first-year experience programs, residential learning communities, writing across the curriculum programs, faculty development centers, service learning programs, and information technology programs that support on-line and distance education classes is an important goal to pursue. Although progress is being made on many campuses, additional work needs to be done so that future generations can consistently benefit from these endeavors.

References

American Association of School Librarians. *Information Power: Building Partnerships for Learning*. Chicago: American Library Association, 1998.

Asselin, Marlene, and Elizabeth Lee. "'I Wish Someone Had Taught Me':
Information Literacy in a Teacher Education Program." *Teacher Librarian*,
Dec. 2002, 30(2), 10–17.

"ACRL Guidelines for Distance Learning Library Services." *College and Research
Libraries News*, 1998, 59(9), 689–694.

Baron, Leora. "Thriving in Academe: Why Information Literacy?" *NEA Higher
Education Advocate Online*, n.d. http://www.nea.org/he/advo01/
advo0108/front.html.

Bean, John C. *Engaging Ideas: The Professor's Guide to Integrating Writing, Critical
Thinking, and Active Learning in the Classroom*. San Francisco: Jossey-Bass,
1996.

Blakeslee, Sarah, and Kristin Johnson. "Using HorizonLive to Deliver Library
Instruction." *Reference Services Review*, 2002, 30(4), 324–329.

Blakeslee, Sarah, Jim Owens, and Lori Dixon. "Chico's First-Year Experience
Course: A Case Study." *Academic Exchange Quarterly*, Winter 2001, 5(4),
128–132.

Boff, Colleen, and Kristin Johnson. "The Library and First-Year Experience
Courses: A Nationwide Study." *Reference Services Review*, 2002, 30(4),
277–287.

California School Library Association. "Strategy 1: Writing/Keeping a Journal."
In *From Library Skills to Information Literacy: Handbook for the 21st Century*. (2nd ed.) San Jose, Calif.: Hi Willow Research and Publishing,
1997, p. 73.

Carr, Jo Ann. "Information Literacy and Teacher Education." ERIC Digest 97–4.
Washington, D.C.: ERIC Clearinghouse on Teaching and Teacher Education, Nov. 1998. (ED 424 231)

Elmborg, James K. "Information Literacy and Writing Across the Curriculum:
Sharing the Vision." *Reference Services Review*, 2003, 31(1), 68–80.

Fenske, Rachel, and Susan Clark. "Incorporating Library Instruction in a General Education Program for College Freshmen." *Reference Services Review*,
1995, 23(3), 69–74.

Gibson, Craig. "Research Skills Across the Curriculum: Connections with
Writing-Across-the-Curriculum." In Jean Sheridan (ed.), *Writing-Across-
the-Curriculum and the Academic Library: A Guide for Librarians, Instructors, and Writing Program Directors*. Westport, Conn.: Greenwood Press,
1995, pp. 55–69.

Iannuzzi, Patricia. "Faculty Development and Information Literacy: Establishing
Campus Partnerships." *Reference Services Review*, Fall–Winter 1998,
26(3/4), 97–102, 116.

Intersegmental Committee of the Academic Senates of the California Community Colleges, the California State University, and the University of California. *Academic Literacy: A Statement of Competencies Expected of Students Entering California's Public Colleges and Universities*. Sacramento: Intersegmental Committee of the Academic Senates of the California Community Colleges, the California State University, and the University of California, Spring 2002. Also available at http://www.academicsenate. cc.ca.us/publications/papers/academicliteracy/main.htm.

Jacobson, Trudi E., and Helene C. Williams. *Teaching the New Library to Today's Users*. New York: Neal-Schuman, 2000.

Jacoby, Barbara. "Building Service Learning Partnerships for the Future." In *Building Partnerships for Service Learning*. San Francisco: Jossey-Bass, 2003, pp. 314–337.

Libutti, Patricia O'Brien, and Bonnie Gratch (eds.). *Teaching Information Retrieval and Evaluation Skills for Education Students and Practitioners: A Casebook of Applications*. Chicago: Association of College and Research Libraries, 1995.

Macklin, Alexius Smith. "Integrating Information Literacy Using Problem-Based Learning." *Reference Services Review*, 2001, 29(4), 306–313.

McLean, Marion S., and Marion M. Mohr. *Teacher Researchers at Work*. Berkeley, Calif.: National Writing Project, 1999.

Nugent, Chris, and Roger Myers. "Learning by Doing: The Freshman-Year Curriculum and Library Instruction." *Research Strategies*, 2000, 17, 147–155.

Paul, Richard, Linda Elder, and Ted Bartell. "Study of 38 Public Universities and 28 Private Universities to Determine Faculty Emphasis on Critical Thinking in Instruction." 2002. http://www.criticalthinking.org/ schoolstudy.htm.

Pierard, Cindy, and Kathryn Graves. "The Greatest Problem with Which the Library Is Confronted: A Survey of Academic Library Outreach to the Freshman Course." In Maurie Caitlin Kelly and Andrea Kross (eds.), *Making the Grade: Academic Libraries and Student Success*. Chicago: Association of College and Research Libraries, 2002, pp. 71–89.

Rader, Hannelore. "Educating Students for the Information Age: The Role of the Librarian." *Reference Services Review*, 1997, 25(2), 47–52.

Riddle, John S. "Where's the Library in Service Learning? Models for Engaged Library Instruction." *Journal of Academic Librarianship*, Mar. 2003, 29(2), 71–81.

Rockman, Ilene. "More Than Faculty Training: Integrating Information Competence into the Disciplines." *College and Research Libraries News,* Mar. 2000, *61*(3), 192–194.

Sensenbaugh, Roger. "Writing Across the Curriculum. Toward the Year 2000. ERIC Digest." Bloomington, IN: ERIC Clearinghouse on Reading and Communication Skills, 1993. (ED 354 549) http://www.ericfacility.net/databases/ERIC_Digests/ed354549.html.)

Sheridan, Jean (ed.). *Writing-Across-the-Curriculum and the Academic Library: A Guide for Librarians, Instructors, and Writing Program Directors.* Westport, Conn.: Greenwood Press, 1995.

St. John, Kelly. "CSU Students Still Need Remedial Help." *San Francisco Chronicle,* Jan. 29, 2003, p. A-15.

Templeton, Lolly, and Signia Warner. "Incorporating Information Literacy into Teacher Education." *Academic Exchange Quarterly,* 2002, *6*(4), 71–76.

Tsui, Lisa. "Faculty Attitudes and the Development of Students' Critical Thinking." *Journal of General Education,* 2001, *50*(1), 1–28.

Werrell, Emily. "The Freshman Year Experience: A Library Component That Works." In Linda Shirato (ed.), *Programs That Work: Papers and Session Materials Presented at the Twenty-Fourth National LOEX Library Instruction Conference.* Ann Arbor, Mich.: Pierian Press, 1997, pp. 169–177.

Young, James B., and Ashley Taliaferro Williams. "The Integration of Information Literacy Skills in a Year-Long Learning Community Program: A Faculty and Librarian Collaboration." In Julia K. Nims, Randal Baier, Rita Bullard, Eric Owens (eds.). *Integrating Information Literacy into the College Experience: Papers Presented at the Thirtieth National LOEX Library Instruction Conference.* Ann Arbor, Mich.: Pierian Press, 2003, pp. 19–24.

Zilius, Pamela, and Deborah Tenofsky. "Remote Real-Time Library Instruction Via Cable Television." *Research Strategies,* 2000, *17*, 231–236.

3

Developing Freshman-Level Tutorials to Promote Information Literacy

Patrick Sullivan

Information literacy efforts on campuses have become more visible recently as campus mission statements have encouraged the expansion of teaching and learning activities. Approaches to integrating information literacy into the higher education curriculum have varied widely from institution to institution, depending on local cultures and needs. A number of efforts have focused on the freshman experience, with the library at the center of the effort, working closely with the general education and first-year experience programs to deliver information literacy instruction.

Due to the large numbers of students that must be reached through these lower-division courses and the importance of reaching them early in their academic career, the use of on-line tutorials to deliver instruction in core information and communication competencies has become commonplace. Students benefit when they have time to learn the fundamental competencies of locating, using, evaluating, and communicating information within the context of course assignments early in their academic career. In addition, having multiple opportunities to reinforce these important skills in lower-division courses allows students to be more successful in their upper-division studies.

Characteristics of First-Year Students and Implications for Tutorials

Most first-year students currently entering colleges and universities were born at about the same time as the Macintosh computer. They grew up with the graphical user interface, mouse, and local area networks. Later, they embraced home on-line information services, chat rooms, cell phones, and school computer labs. Today, they also benefit from the ability to check out wireless devices, such as laptop computers, from their academic libraries in support of their ubiquitous computing needs.

Referred to as "Generation Y," "Echo Boomers," "the Plug-and-Play Generation," "the Net Generation," "Millenials," "the Game Boy Generation," among other monikers, they are undoubtedly a much more technically sophisticated generation than previous generations. These students come to higher education ready to accept on-line tutorials that deliver specific content within a self-paced, interactive, individualized instructional environment. They appreciate the fact that these tutorials can be programmed to give immediate feedback and are available twenty-four hours a day, seven days a week.

Keeping the prospective users in mind is essential in the development of on-line tutorials. Conversations with tutorial developers reveal that one differentiating factor between the so-so and the sublime is the level of faculty and student involvement in the initial design of the tutorial. Without this vital insight into the process and perceptions of first-year students, one can run the risk of creating a tutorial with little relevance for its intended audience.

Lorie Roth (1999) in her article, "Educating the Cut-and-Paste Generation," has observed that for freshman students "the visual image—not the word—is the primary means of communication and the unifying cultural force" (p. 42). Adding to Roth's observation on visual imagery is the fact that a full-featured multimedia experience—music, graphics, and video—is the preferred learning and entertainment experience for many of these students. This has clear implications for developers. Compared with a text-and-graphics tutorial, not only does the hardware and software required for a high-end multimedia tutorial increase in complexity, but the technical skills needed on the development team must also be ratcheted up.

Another typical characteristic of today's student is a seemingly native ability to multitask. It is not unusual to view a student at the information commons speaking on a cell phone, sending off an instant message, and completing a research paper, all at the same time. Clearly this generation of students can handle the nonlinear approach to information literacy, and developers need to explore how best to create the diverse paths from which these students can select.

Librarians must also critically examine this multitasking phenomenon, because as the Pew Internet & American Life project reports, while "students as a group have grown up using tools such as instant messaging, chat rooms and electronic mail, little has been done to determine the effect . . . academically, on college students" (Jones, 2002).

The questions for developers become "Can some of these new communication paradigms be integrated into on-line efforts? Are there facets of instant messaging and on-line chats that can provide a more collaborative learning experience within our tutorials?" A frequent concern of developers is how to get students into simulated or live search environments via a second browser window without overloading them with too many stimuli and too much information. Perhaps, given the propensity of today's students for multitasking, the problem is not one of limiting the use of multiwindow scenarios but rather ensuring that there are clear navigational cues between the different tasks.

What is Good Instruction in an Electronic Environment?

Nancy Dewald (1999a) provides a discussion of best practices for Web-based information literacy instruction. She observes that many of these points are transferable to on-line tutorials and uses them to evaluate a number of tutorial efforts.

- Instruction is best received when it is course-related and, more specifically, assignment-related. Such instruction will contribute to greater retention of material and an increased level of student motivation for learning than if it were given in isolation.

- Active learning incorporated into instruction is more effective than one-way communication such as a lecture. Having information reinforced through exercises or activities engages students in the learning process. Ridgeway (1989) concurs: "Research has also shown that active learning activities are more effective at achieving higher cognitive objectives than are passive learning situations."

- Collaborative learning can be beneficial, because it encourages students to work together to solve problems and critically analyze material. The interactive technologies available via on-line tutorials can provide fresh and stimulating ways for students to work with information literacy concepts. While on-line tutorials often seem to isolate users rather than encourage interaction, special features such as "group meeting rooms" that simulate the chat and instant messaging environments that students already warmly embrace can accomplish this collaborative learning/social interaction goal.

- Information provided in more than one format can be helpful, because students have different learning styles. Thus when text and visuals are combined, powerful learning can result.

- Establishing clear objectives is important, so that students easily follow the direction of the instruction.

- It is best to teach concepts rather than mechanics, so that students can transfer their learning from course to course. When students understand how to search for and evaluate information resources, they will become more confident learners.

Dewald's points reinforce the ones by Chickering and Gamson's "Seven Principles for Good Practice in Undergraduate Education," published by the American Association for Higher Education. Although they were published in 1987, the seven principles can readily be applied to a contemporary on-line learning environment. Chickering and Gamson (1987) note that good practice

- Encourages contact between faculty and students; this important learning characteristic can be achieved in the design of on-line tutorials by having the program output student scores to the professor

- Develops reciprocity and cooperation among students; this can be accomplished on-line through the inclusion of collaborative exercises

- Uses active learning, which helps students to deepen understanding, internalize knowledge, and readily apply it to any new learning situation, including those which are in an on-line environment

- Gives prompt feedback, which helps students to focus their learning and immediately correct misunderstandings or mistakes; this is a common characteristic of interactive on-line tutorial programs

- Emphasizes time on task, a factor that students can take responsibility for by completing assigned work efficiently and effectively, twenty-four hours a day in an on-line environment

- Communicates high expectations, an important characteristic in any learning environment

- Respects diverse talents and ways of learning; this is a strength of on-line tutorials

By continuing to focus on the importance of good teaching practices, on-line tutorials can be developed for freshman users to advance their information literacy competencies.

Useful Design Issues to Consider

Building on the characteristics of good undergraduate education, image-based teaching materials can be created when developers follow appropriate design characteristics and models.

Smith (2001) observes that since "the Web has become an everyday part of most libraries' delivery of services" (p. 1), it is a perfect platform for delivering information literacy instruction. In addition, Boff and Johnson (2002, p. 277) note that "first-year experience courses are excellent venues for introducing freshmen students to information literacy concepts." Before embarking on a Web-based project of this magnitude, however, it is important to establish a design and development plan to ensure that appropriate goals and objectives are met within a reasonable time frame. Planning for all phases of the project, from pre-production to evaluation, will maximize resources. Factors to consider in the pre-production phase include a thorough needs analysis, with input from both faculty and students. Based on the needs analysis, it will be possible to move with confidence to design, prototyping, production, testing, revising, evaluating, marketing, and maintenance phases. As part of the design phase, particular attention should be given to the following elements:

- *User interface:* This is the entry point for students and thus is critical to engaging them in the learning process and motivating them to continue as independent learners.

- *Navigation strategies:* These must be logical and user-centered, so that students do not become lost before they interact with the content to be learned.

- *Multimedia features:* Increased learning and retention can occur when the right balance is struck between graphics, sound, animation, and video.

Exemplary Tutorial Sites

Several sources provide listings of information literacy tutorials. These include those provided by the Internet Education Project (http://cooley.colgate.edu/etech/iep/default.html), the Library Instruction Round Table (http://www3.baylor.edu/LIRT/lirtinte. html), and the Library Orientation Exchange (http://www.emich. edu/public/loex/islinks/tutlinks.htm). In addition, Johnson (2003) has compiled an extensive list of information literacy tutorials that have been developed by universities during the past few years and has categorized them according to their support of information literacy competencies. Of the more than one hundred listed, some are truly exemplary, having received peer recognition for their solid pedagogical approach to learning, stylish graphics, interactivity, and sustainability. Some of these exemplary tutorials are described in the following sections.

University of Texas System

The Texas Information Literacy Tutorial (TILT, http://tilt.lib.ut system.edu/), which was created by the University of Texas system, is probably the most widely known information literacy tutorial today. In 2000, TILT received the Innovation Award from the Instruction Section of the Association of College and Research Libraries. Committee members specifically cited the tutorial's "sound learning theory . . . transferability of research and critical thinking skills . . . truly interactive and personalized learning environment; and . . . appropriate use of graphics and humor" (Association of College and Research Libraries, 2002). Because of the efforts of the Digital Information Literacy Office of the University of Texas system in disseminating information about TILT, interactive tutorial development within higher education has been greatly influenced by this excellent model.

What users experience when exploring the TILT site is the result of years of development efforts and attention to detail. From the opening screen, where the options of TILT Lite (no plug-ins required) or Full TILT (Shockwave Flash required) are presented, users notice that the developers have targeted flexibility. This flexible approach, according to the developer, allows access for those with slower dial-up connections and provides some level of compliance with the Americans with Disabilities Act requirement to make electronic information accessible to those users with disabilities. The pages generally fit on a single screen with minimal scrolling required, and the mix of graphics and text creates a balance that is easy for the user to read and navigate.

The TILT site also has a module called "Current Internet Issues" that allows the user to select from six different Internet issues and then inserts appropriate examples for the rest of that section. This modular, personalized approach to tutorial development makes it relevant to students, and it provides an excellent example of customization for subsequent developers to follow.

In addition, the TILT site is impressive for offering the TILT Open Publication License. This license allows other institutions to save valuable time and energy by using the TILT modules and programming code to create their own customized versions of the tutorial. At this writing, there are nineteen sites from Australia to the Netherlands that have implemented the TILT code on their campus. While many institutions have simply changed the names and colors to represent their own institution, there are others, such as

Searchpath (http://www.wmich.edu/library/searchpath) at Western Michigan University (WMU), that have borrowed a little and built a lot. WMU has incorporated the TILT code but has added its own navigational changes, graphics, and modules, including an excellent module on plagiarism. Following the example of the TILT team and its Open Publication License, the Searchpath tutorial program was made available for download from the WMU site in June 2002.

California Polytechnic State University, San Luis Obispo

Cal Poly San Luis Obispo has built another site (http://www.lib. calpoly.edu/infocomp/modules/index.html) that reflects both a high level of technical expertise and a collaborative development model. The Cal Poly effort started in 1996 as part of the California State University's Information Competence Initiative. As with the TILT site, Cal Poly has created an easily navigable tutorial with eye-catching graphics, engaging activities, and reinforcing exercises that students remember. The Cal Poly site was also recognized by the Association of College and Research Libraries in 1998 as one of the top ten tutorials of the year. Cal Poly shares the commitment to open source code, and over the years numerous sites have built upon its original offerings.

San Francisco State University

San Francisco State University (SFSU) has a long history of information literacy on campus. The university had previously required completion of a workbook as part of its information literacy graduation requirement. The workbook was turned into an on-line interactive tutorial (http://oasis.sfsu.edu/), influenced by the Cal Poly model, and students are now required to complete the Online Advancement of Student Information Skills (OASIS) tutorial. OASIS gives undergraduate students a basic level of competence in the skills needed to find, use, and evaluate information of all kinds. Successful completion of the tutorial is required of all first-year students by the end of their first year and of all incoming transfer students by the end of their first semester at SFSU. The tutorial consists of eight chapters, each of which is followed by a short quiz that students take on-line. Quizzes are automatically graded on-line, and the results are simultaneously displayed on the student's monitor and recorded in the student record.

One interesting facet of the development and implementation of the OASIS tutorial is the dedication by library management of $2,000 to facilitate the successful marketing of the project to both students and faculty across campus (Rosen and Castro, 2002). The marketing of tutorial developments is an area that is too often overlooked or minimized and that can substantially affect the overall success of a program.

Griffith University

Another site that took advantage of the generosity of Cal Poly in sharing its tutorial development is Griffith University in Australia, which uses the tutorial on six campuses (http://www4.gu.edu.au/shr/lrt/). Griffith's path to a Web-based program was similar to that of San Francisco State University in that it began with a printed workbook. They modified the Cal Poly tutorial, adding an updated, more appealing graphic look, as well as an orientation that uses the research process as its organizational model. They also included a requirement that the Shockwave plug-in be installed, as well as the Quick Time plug-in, should a user decide to access the video module within the communication section of the tutorial.

LILI: the Learn Information Literacy Initiative of South Australia

Winner of the inaugural South Australian Training Initiative Award in 2002, the LILI site (http://www.tafe.sa.edu.au/lili/) was created by the LEARN Network of South Australian Technical and Further Education (TAFE) Libraries. The site states the following principles:

- Every person has the right to opportunities to acquire the skills, knowledge, and understanding to assess, evaluate, and use information effectively.

- Equitable access to an information literacy program should be ensured for all students.

- At the heart of information literacy are people who are able to engage with their information world.

- On-line information literacy materials provide students with the knowledge and understanding to enable them to make informed judgments about how to access, evaluate, and use on-line information.

The tutorial provides excellent guidance for students on how to analyze their assignments and then search, find, evaluate, and cite information sources. Clean graphics and text inform students of what they should be able to do after completing a module, and there are ample opportunities to click on a menu for help or take a private quiz to assess one's knowledge of the subject matter.

Other Tutorial Sites

There are a wealth of other exemplary sites that warrant review. One of these is "Information Literacy and You" (http://www.libraries.psu.edu/crsweb/infolit/andyou/infoyou.htm) from Pennsylvania State University. The opening screen of this tutorial does many things well. It graphically demonstrates the ordered steps in the traditional research process and allows users to step into the process at any point. This permits professors to more easily assign one portion of the tutorial to a class when all they need, for example, is the section that provides instruction on how to cite a source. The opening screen also incorporates effective rollovers (buttons that change as the mouse rolls over them) that give just enough information without either overwhelming the user or providing too little information. In addition, there is a topic list and index to the site, suggestions for faculty on incorporating the site's material into their classes, and credits that provide insight into how the site came to be. The site also incorporates a research log in which students can record notes or observations and e-mail them to their professor or to themselves. All of these functions are accomplished via graphically pleasing, uncluttered screens. Throughout the tutorial, the authors provide clear navigational cues that are guided by youthful, ghostlike characters. The content of this site is neatly packaged into concise modules through which users can easily move with minimal scrolling. In all, this is an attractive and effective site.

Another site that merits examination is the Data Game site from Colorado State University (CSU) (http://lib.colostate.edu/datagame/). This site was created using Macromedia's Authorware software, and mimics a traditional game show, using interesting animation. The animated characters, Dewey Knowitall, Coach Chuck Lugnut, Gloria Gownwell, and Ali the robot, provide an amusing and informative session for students working their way through the four modules. Using the game show metaphor provides students with an interactive and fun learning experience. Polly Thistlewaite (2001) observes that the developers made conscious decisions to include CSU-specific instruction and to require that the tutorial be run over a high-speed connection. Although current students have grown up with animation in popular television shows and feature-length films, Data Game's extensive use of this medium is unique in today's tutorial development environment. Each module in Data Game contains a contest that students must complete or else face the prospect of repeating the game. Scores from the Big Daddy Quiz can be sent to instructors who have chosen to incorporate this tutorial into their classes.

Purdue University has developed an innovative tutorial that also deserves recognition (http://core.lib.purdue.edu/). The site, Comprehensive Online Research Education (CORE), provides an exemplary overview of the research process with some special features. The developers have done an excellent job of providing an overview of the objectives, not just at the beginning of the tutorial but also in each of the subsections. The graphics and the layout of the navigation panels are concise and easily understood. In addition to quizzes that allow users to assess their knowledge of concepts, the tutorial has a live on-line practice session that does an excellent job of prompting the user through the split-screen scenario without losing or confusing them. One of the more impressive features in this tutorial is the module called "Plan Your Project." The developers explain in detail how students should divide their time when approaching a term paper project. This in itself might not seem so remarkable, but the tutorial also provides a project planner module in which the student can enter a start date and a due date, and the module will then create a detailed project timeline. Because many freshmen have difficulty with time management, this is an especially important feature.

The Gelman Library at George Washington University has developed a tutorial especially for freshman advising to help the transition from high school to college. The Freshman Advising Workshop Library Tutorial (http://www.gwu.edu/gelman/instruct/faw/intro/) is an interactive tutorial designed to show incoming freshmen the basics of searching the library catalogue and specific databases such as Lexis-Nexis and Periodical Abstracts. The goal of the tutorial, according to the authors, is to "provide hands-on experience in searching the catalog and databases." With this in mind, the tutorial employs Javascript and other DHTML tools to create mock-ups of search interfaces. Students interact with these mock-ups in order to complete the tutorial.

Across the Atlantic, the European Union has funded a project titled "Internet Detective" (http://www.sosig.ac.uk/desire/internet-detective.html), a multilingual English, French, and Dutch interactive tutorial on evaluating the quality of Internet resources. The tutorial has been incorporated into a number of classes, either as an on-line presentation or via the exercises that are part of the tutorial. Internet Detective incorporates a simple registration system that allows students to return to the area where they left off. The entire site can be downloaded, and it also contains a guide that helps instructors understand how the different modules can be used to support their classes. In addition, the tutorial package includes a PowerPoint presentation that can be used to introduce the tutorial to students or faculty, a marketing item not often included in other such projects. While not the most technologically sophisticated of today's tutorial offerings, Internet Detective is a very pragmatic solution that has found a home in a number of different classes around the globe.

Challenges in Developing On-Line Tutorials

There are several challenges for universities and developers to consider at the beginning of an information literacy tutorial project. First, there is the *process* challenge. While different models for the design process may be selected, it is imperative that a formalized process exist from the outset if a quality product is to be developed. This most critical part of the process will ensure success only if realistic timelines and deliverables are established. A poor plan, even with all the right resources, will not deliver a quality product. Generally, the use of a project management software package such as Microsoft Project will greatly aid in visualizing the project in its entirety, including the human resources needed to complete required tasks, the dependencies linking group members, and the overall timeline. This will help everyone to stay energized through what may be a very lengthy process.

Assumptions present another challenge, especially when they have not been validated. There is no substitute for focus groups and usability testing when trying to discern the preferences of first-year students or the effectiveness of a given instructional scenario. It is difficult for even the youngest developers to know the mind-set of a freshman student. Assumptions must constantly be tested and retested. Veldof and Beavers (2001) observe that "libraries need to situate information literacy education within a mental model that works for students, and not one that simply suits librarians."

Resource challenges relate back to the initial process challenge. The fact that the process has been mapped out and funds have all been allocated does not guarantee that events will not change. Build flexibility into the process, so that if a problem is encountered, resources can be reallocated or the project can be scaled back. This is clearly preferable to continuing with unrealistic goals or insufficient resources. Regularly checking in with team members ensures that each group has the resources needed and that everyone still has the same end result in mind.

Another major challenge for developers is *evaluation*. Tutorial development includes time-consuming, skill-intensive activities that stretch the boundaries of what has traditionally been taught in information and computer science programs. Instructional designers and assessment experts need to be brought into the process to provide expertise. Being able to assess a student's development means having an accurate picture of the starting skill set and which changes are attributable to the tutorial intervention. It is easy to see why evaluative challenges can sometimes be the thorniest and why they should be addressed at the very earliest stages of the project plan. The most graphically intriguing tutorial, while attractive to students, will be of little use if it cannot demonstrate to students and administrators what was accomplished.

The final challenge is the *institutional* challenge. Creating and maintaining an information literacy program and, as one facet of that program, an on-line tutorial will require solid institutional commitment and bona fide institutional effort. This will mean, in many cases, systematic reallocation of resources, moving away from the traditional division between various groups of employees toward interdepartmental teams working together with a common goal and with a realization that information literacy is a major priority for the organization. Having a solid plan, including long-term implementation strategies and a realistic understanding on the part of administrators and team members about what can be accomplished, will lead to a successful tutorial project.

Expertise Needed

A basic understanding of software technologies is required to develop a successful tutorial. Just as tutorials are located on a continuum from the very simple to the exceptionally complicated, so too are the technologies they employ. Javascript, PHP, Flash, Director, XML, Authorware, ColdFusion—the range of technologies and programs at work in some of today's tutorials can be mind-boggling. There may also be a learning curve for hardware, especially if one is not familiar with digital video cameras, drawing tablets, scanners, and other tools that allow graphic designers to catch the eye of today's undergraduate students and satisfy their need for visually stimulating on-line experiences.

Another aspect that tutorial developers need to consider is the move by many campuses to expand use of course management software systems such as Blackboard (http://www.blackboard.com) and WebCT (http://www.webct.com). It may be possible to take advantage of the tools provided by these vendors for quiz generation, randomization of quiz questions, collaborative group spaces, and statistical reporting capabilities.

Future Directions

As can be seen from the earlier review of exemplary tutorial sites, there are many ways in which even the most successful sites can be improved. The possibilities for future on-line tutorials are even more incredible, given rapidly emerging technologies.

The developers of the TILT tutorial have outlined some of the possibilities that they envision (Dupuis, 2001). These included changes in

- Quizzes: Within TILT, the quizzes are designed to specifically test the skills outlined at the beginning of each module. With additional programming, a variety of questions could be designed so the quiz asks different question each time.

- Statistics: Statistics pages within TILT are functional but basic. Improvements could be made to make monitoring of statistics less time-consuming and comparison over time easier.

- Interactions: Interactions are most effective when they are personalized to an individual's level of knowledge and interests.

- Individually generated tutorials, additional modules, discipline-specific modules

- Translations: Libraries from a variety of countries have proposed translating TILT into different languages, offering some interesting possibilities for new international collaborations.

Personalization and Customization

Nancy Dewald (1999b) notes, "Web elements . . . allow librarians to create Web-based instruction that allows students to explore as they prefer." Users can customize the tutorials to use their preferred learning styles or address particular areas of interest. A future scenario might include a pretest that both assesses the individual's preferred learning style (auditory, visual, tactile, or a combination) and probes areas of interest. Customization of the tool might occur similar to the way that users are presented with customized ads depending on what they entered into a Web search engine.

Personalization will allow developers to use the core of a tutorial with interchangeable, discipline-specific modules targeting different education levels or majors. Tutorials can be scaled from freshman to senior levels. In addition, they can be programmed to remember a student's name and preferences upon log-in, welcoming them back to the exact spot where they left off. Tools are also available to test language proficiency, an important feature for many institutions that serve a diverse student population. On-line tutorial designers may find it desirable to use readability indexes for sentence length and complexity of vocabulary, just as textbook publishers do.

Modularity

A flexible, modular approach to learning information literacy principles will attract the widest number of users. Kelly Donaldson (2000) has observed that "breaking down instruction tutorials into manageable sections (modules) while remaining linear and allowing for the step-by-step acquisition of skills, prevents the user from becoming overwhelmed with information." It also allows maximum flexibility for developers. Warren Longmire (2000) points out that reusable learning objects (RLOs) can prove useful by providing "modular, freestanding, and transportable" solutions. This might mean, for example, that an on-line catalogue search segment that was developed for a business tutorial could be plugged into a science tutorial with few changes, if any. This not only ensures consistency but allows for easy integration of modules into a complete tutorial package.

Video Images

With the increases in network bandwidth and the propensity of freshman students to choose video learning, video elements may appear more frequently in future multimedia tutorials. Recently, John Hickok (2002) of California State University, Fullerton, created some excellent library tours of the Pollak Library that incorporate a mix of all the right elements (http://library.fullerton.edu/tour/). The video tours have clean, crisp graphics; professional transitions; young student actors; and speech patterns that resonate with today's students. Users are offered multiple viewer options (Quick Time, Real Player or Media Player) and multiple compression schemes for remote or locally connected users.

There are a number of ways that video technology can be woven into future development efforts; for example, video footage can be used to model desired student behavior, or it can also be used as part of a quiz in which students might be asked to piece together separate video scenes into a properly sequenced research process or search strategy session.

Other streaming video efforts include a visual library instructional tour created by the University of Tennessee (http://yucca. lib.utk.edu/video/hodgesQT.html) and the DataLine BG streaming video newscast (http://www.bgsu.edu/colleges/library/infosrv/lue/ dataline.html) created by Bowling Green State University. This site includes in its newscast a piece called "Research Stress Syndrome" and a clip called "Talking to a Database," as well as more traditional sections such as "Finding Articles" and "Finding Books."

Media plug-ins required to view these videos have already become more transparent to users, and such technical issues will likely be even less of a consideration for future developers.

Interactivity

Many of the exemplary tutorials use interactivity in simulations, quizzes, and assorted exercises. In the future, more of these types of quizzes will appear, with ever more sophisticated interfaces, easier methods for randomization of questions, and greater breadth of media types. The reporting systems for letting students know how they scored will undoubtedly also become much more graphical in the future.

Mimicking the multitasking capabilities of students, there could be mock instant message interruptions during a module that introduce a snap quiz or deliver additional information on a given topic when students' scores indicate that they have not understood a concept or critically analyzed an information passage.

Assessment

As new tutorial efforts begin to build on the lessons learned from their predecessors, not only will more sophisticated tutorials appear, incorporating cutting-edge technologies, but assessment will also assume an expanded role. While there are already information literacy assessment projects under way, these have not made their way into individual tutorial efforts very quickly. As alliances grow between tutorial developers and assessment experts, quiz results may begin to better address the gaps in student knowledge. For example, rather than receiving a message noting that 75 percent of the questions were answered correctly, a student might receive a conceptual map of the tutorial results, showing the sections and subsections where he or she did well and the ones where additional work is needed.

Summary

Information literacy should be woven throughout a student's entire academic career, using a variety of instructional approaches. A growing instructional strategy, especially for freshman courses, is the on-line tutorial. Knowledge of how first-year students acquire information is the first step toward successful tutorial development.

Creating lively, interactive sessions while holding true to the goal of transmitting information literacy information is a challenge. Ideally, it can be done creatively, and students can be incorporated in all phases of development. Tapscott (1998) observes that educational technology "will grow from the rich experience of students working with teachers to forge, through actual experience, a new model of learning." By building on the solid foundation of existing instructional practices and integrating promising technologies in the future, developers can craft a new wave of information literacy tutorials that address the important competencies required for all freshmen to become lifelong learners.

References

Association of College and Research Libraries, Instruction Section. "Innovation in Instruction Award Winners." 2002. http://www/ala.org/acrl/is/awards/innovation-winners.html. Accessed Nov. 12, 2002.

Boff, Colleen, and Kristen Johnson. "The Library and First-Year Experience Courses: A Nationwide Study." *Reference Services Review,* 2002, 30(4), 277–287.

Chickering, Arthur W., and Zelda F. Gamson. "Seven Principles for Good Practice in Undergraduate Education," *AAHE Bulletin*, Mar. 1987, pp. 3–7.

Dewald, Nancy H. "Transporting Good Library Instruction Practices into the Web Environment: An Analysis of Online Tutorials." *Journal of Academic Librarianship*, 1999a, *25*(1), 26–32.

Dewald, Nancy H. "Web-Based Library Instruction: What Is Good Pedagogy?" *Information Technology and Libraries*, 1999b, *18*(1), 26–31.

Donaldson, Kelly A. "Library Research Success: Designing an Online Tutorial to Teach Information Literacy Skills to First-Year Students." *The Internet and Higher Education*, 2000, *2*(4), 237–251.

Dupuis, Elizabeth. "Development Possibilities." March 2001. http://tilt.lib. utsystem.edu/yourtilt/docs/development.html. Accessed Nov. 17, 2002.

Hickock, John. "Web Library Tours: Using Streaming Video and Interactive Quizzes." *Reference Services Review*, 2002, *30*(2), 99–111.

Johnson, Corey. "Information Literacy Library Tutorials – Master List. General, Discipline Specific, and Resource Specific." 2003. http://www.wsulibs. wsu.edu/usered/tutorials/tutorialslist.html.

Jones, Steve. "The Internet Goes to College: How Students Are Living in the Future with Today's Technology." Sept. 15, 2002. http://www.pewinter net.org/reports/toc.asp?Report=71. Accessed Oct. 20, 2002.

Longmire, Warren. "A Primer on Learning Objects." Mar. 2000. http://www. learningcircuits.org/mar2000/primer.html. Accessed Nov. 10, 2002.

Ridgeway, Trish. "Integrating Active Learning Techniques into the One-Hour Bibliographic Lecture." In Glenn E. Mensching and Teresa B. Mensching (eds.), *Coping With Information Illiteracy: Bibliographic Instruction for the Information Age*. Ann Arbor, Mich.: Pierian Press, 1989, pp. 33–36.

Rosen, Jeff, and Gina M. Castro. "From Workbook to Web: Building an Information Literacy Oasis." *Computers in Libraries*, 2002, *22*(1), 30–35.

Roth, Lorie. "Educating the Cut-and-Paste Generation." *Library Journal*, Nov. 1, 1999, *124*(18) 42-44.

Smith, Susan Sharpless. *Web-Based Instruction: A Guide for Libraries*. Chicago: American Library Association, 2001.

Tapscott, Don. *Growing Up Digital: The Rise of the Net Generation*. New York: McGraw-Hill, 1998.

Thistlewaite, Polly. "The Data Game: Colorado State University's Animated Library Research Tutorial." *Colorado Libraries*, 2001, *27*(3), 12–15.

Veldof, Jerilyn, and Karen Beavers. "Going Mental: Tackling Mental Models for the Online Library." *Research Strategies*, 2001, *18*, 3–20.

4

Integrating Information Competence into an Interdisciplinary Major

Pam Baker, Renée R. Curry

Background: The Human Communication Degree at CSU Monterey Bay

The print and on-line catalogue for the Human Communication Bachelor of Arts degree in the Institute for Human Communication, California State University Monterey Bay, opens philosophically: "In this era of multiculturalism, social transformations, and new technologies, humanists involved in interdisciplinary studies will play a more important role than ever before. They will bring cultural, creative, critical, and historical understanding to problem solving. They will model ethical and humane communication. Experts in culture, communication, and creative expression will be the pillars of this new millennium" (California State University, Monterey Bay, 2002a, 2002b, p. 42).

The philosophy of this major becomes even more explicit in the Institute for Human Communication's mission statement, which describes the program goals toward preparation of "ethical, creative, and critical thinker[s] and doer[s] in a multicultural and increasingly interconnected global society" (California State University, Monterey Bay, 2002a, 2002b, p. 42). It also expresses the major as an interdisciplinary humanities major that "integrates the traditional disciplines of literature, history, philosophy, rhetoric, communication, journalism, media studies, and creative writing with the contemporary fields of ethnic studies (Chicana/Latina/African American, Asian American, Euro American, Native American), American studies, women's studies, cultural studies, and media studies" (California State University, Monterey Bay, 2002a, 2002b, p. 42). The faculty, who developed this mission statement and who deliver this curriculum and degree program, take seriously the commitment to the provision of an interdisciplinary program in critical and applied learning.

The program delivered in the Institute for Human Communication visibly and unapologetically grapples with the ambiguity inherent in any interdisciplinary curriculum. As interdisciplinary scholar Joe Moran reminds us, "This ambiguity is partly reflected in the slipperiness of the term 'interdisciplinary.' It can suggest forging connections across the different disciplines; but it can also mean establishing a kind of undisciplined space in the interstices between disciplines, or even attempting to transcend disciplinary boundaries altogether" (Moran, 2002, p. 15). The human communication (HCOM) program at California State University Monterey Bay (CSUMB) often connects differing disciplines, sometimes establishes undisciplined space, and frequently transcends boundaries, but one thing the curriculum always does, in every single course, is deliver student opportunities to attain major learning outcomes and information competencies. The primary point of this chapter is to discuss how infusion and integration of information competencies occurs in a highly articulated, outcomes-based interdisciplinary curriculum.

The university itself is a comprehensive state university that serves "the diverse people of California, especially the working class and historically undereducated and low-income populations" (California State University, Monterey Bay, 2002a, 2002b, p. 4). The university has a tremendous commitment to "multilingual, multicultural, gender-equitable learning" (California State University, Monterey Bay, 2002a, 2002b, p. 4). CSUMB offers an outcomes-based learning environment across the campus, which means that the "desired end results are identified first, and then the means to achieve those results are identified and developed" (California State University, Monterey

Bay, 2002a, 2002b, p. 15). The faculty articulate learning outcomes and assessment activities required for the major in each course and then develop and implement innovative teaching pedagogies related to student attainment and demonstration of the outcomes. The entire campus curriculum is taught in this way, which creates a powerful learning environment for the students. The students know that they are learning, what they are learning, how they are learning, and why they are learning. Throughout each course and in senior capstone courses, faculty assess whether students are learning. The entire process of learning is visible to and affected by the student.

Information Competency and the California State University System

National and international recognition of information literacy, or information competency, as a crucial skill for students in higher education has been established over the last five to ten years (Bruce, 2000). The American Library Association Presidential Committee on Information Literacy released a report in 1989 on the importance of information literacy (American Library Association, 1989). Following that report, the Association of College and Research Libraries (ACRL) (2000) developed a set of national standards for information literacy. The finalized standards were approved in January 2000 and subsequently endorsed by the American Association for Higher Education. In October 2000, the Council of Australian University Librarians (CAUL) adopted seven standards for information literacy in Australia. The first edition of the CAUL standards was derived from the ACRL information literacy standards (Council of Australian University Librarians, 2001).

A review of the literature on information literacy in higher education indicates a long-standing awareness of the importance of incorporating information literacy skills into the curriculum on many levels and a sustained belief in the importance of faculty-librarian cooperation and collaboration. Numerous studies and reports outline projects in which information literacy skills have been incorporated into individual course assignments across academic disciplines such as composition, psychology, arts, sciences, and nursing (Gauss and King, 1998; Daugherty and Carter, 1997; Atkins, 2001; Brown and Krumholz, 2002; Dorner and Taylor, 2001).

Within the California State University system, there are a growing number of collaborative efforts between librarians and faculty to infuse information literacy outcomes into individual courses (California State University, 2002; Curzon, 2002). California Polytechnic State University, for instance, has developed a list of ten core competencies to be mastered by all students; they have also developed a process by which discipline-specific competencies can be identified (California Polytechnic State University, 2001).

The Association of College and Research Libraries' Institute for Information Literacy (2002) states, "Information literacy includes . . . a set of generic skills and concepts as well as skills and concepts which are specific to certain disciplines and subject areas." A smaller body of literature has begun to address efforts to integrate information literacy standards at the disciplinary major or department level (Humboldt State University, 2002; California State University Long Beach, 2002: San Jose State University, 2001; California State University San Marcos, 2002). However, very few studies have addressed collaborative faculty-librarian efforts to incorporate information literacy outcomes into an interdisciplinary major. One notable example was a project developed at California State University Fullerton (CSUF) in 1999 to "systematically assess acquisition of information competence skills among students enrolled in courses taught within five of the seven colleges on the CSUF campus" (California State University Fullerton, 1999).

An important component of the CSUF project was the collaboration between library faculty with subject expertise and discipline faculty to discuss the integration of information competence objectives, which were expanded or modified to accommodate additional course-related objectives (California State University Fullerton, 1999).

The California State University Information Competency Grant Initiative

In response to the overwhelming interest in information competency within the California State University system, the Chancellor's Office provided resources for the systemwide Information Competency Grant Initiative in spring 2001. Renée Curry, a professor at CSU Monterey Bay, having worked on information competency with librarian Gabriela Sonntag at her previous CSU campus in San Marcos, decided to seek collaboration with CSU Monterey Bay librarians Bill Robnett and Pam Baker in order to submit a grant proposal under the Information Competency Grant Initiative.

A paraphrase of the proposal highlights the two stages of our proposed project: (1) the information competency retreat and (2) the major learning outcome/information competency case studies:

> The Institute for Human Communication at California State University Monterey Bay is an outcomes-based, interdisciplinary humanities institute. Fourteen full-time, tenure-track faculty and ten adjunct faculty with expertise in philosophy, English, creative writing, rhetoric, history, communication, linguistics, women's studies, cultural studies, African American studies, journalism, Chicano/Chicana studies, Latino/Latina studies, and film studies are comprised in the institute. In each of our courses, we assess one or two major learning outcomes that have been designed by the entire institute. Through individual and aggregate portfolios, as well as through senior capstone projects and presentations, we assess eight major learning outcomes—critical communication skills, research analysis, relational communication skills, philosophical analysis, critical cultural analysis, comparative literary analysis, historical analysis, and creative writing and social action—for every graduate of the institute.

The information competency initiative that I am proposing for the Institute for Human Communication at CSU Monterey Bay involves participation of the entire institute, along with leadership and participation by our librarians, at a two-day retreat in fall 2001. The most significant goals of the retreat work are to infuse information competencies into the institute's major learning outcomes, to articulate in writing exactly which information competencies will be achieved as part of the institute's major learning outcomes, and to develop assessment activities that will render student knowledge more visible to us. Through thorough examination of the interconnections among the information competencies and our eight major learning outcomes, and through the development of learning activities, we will deliver curricula that provide ongoing practice with the development of information competencies. It is imperative that the entire institute faculty be involved, because the major learning outcomes are requirements for all the students and because the major learning outcomes are all intricately involved with one another.

At this retreat, we will designate the courses best suited to satisfying particular information competencies; we will also develop course activities and assignments suited to the pedagogy and learning outcomes of the specific courses. Overall, of course, we are most interested in assuring that our students are information competent when they graduate. During this retreat, we will not only analyze syllabi that highlight the competency activities, assignments, and pedagogies, but we will also study and expand our current assessment tools to include the measurement of student information competency skills. Our goal at the retreat in this regard is twofold: (1) to analyze and adapt state, national, and international information competency standards to our curriculum and (2) to integrate appropriate information competencies with our major learning outcomes.

The spring semester will be our case study semester. Case study work groups, centered on single major learning outcomes, will meet twice a month with Renée Curry, director of the Institute for Human Communication, and Bill Robnett and Pam Baker, librarians, for discussion and revision of our individual information competency goals as they relate to our major learning outcomes. At the end of the semester, we will have a set of activities, assignments, and assess ment tools to be tested in classrooms in fall 2002. We will also develop a Web site that communicates our work in information com petency and that solicits further discussion and analysis of our endeavors. [Baker and Curry, 2002, p. 1]

On May 11, 2001, the CSU Information Competency Commit tee awarded us grant monies to support our proposal for the entire academic year.

Grant Implementation Planning Sessions

Library instruction coordinator Pam Baker, library director Bill Robnett, and institute director Renée Curry designed and facili tated the Human Communication Information Competency Retreat. We wanted to create an interactive pedagogical venture into information competency, especially as it related to our inter disciplinary humanities degree. The retreat engaged faculty in the following goals:

- Increased understanding regarding the history of infor mation competency (national, state, and CSU)

- Increased recognition of existing implementations of information competency on the CSUMB campus

- Increased awareness about the parameters of the grant initiative

- Collaborative activities needed to align our institute's learning outcomes with the CSU approved information competencies

The retreat was only the initial stage of the grant activities. The second stage involved faculty participation in analytical case studies throughout the year with the goal of articulating information competencies in all of the HCOM syllabi.

Retreat Activities

The purpose of the two-day Human Communication Information Competency Retreat was to develop collaboration among the human communication faculty regarding the delivery of information competencies to the major.

The conference participants included part-time faculty in journalism, English communication, literature, history, and interpersonal communication, as well as full-time, tenure-track faculty in oral history, Latino/Latina studies, philosophy, communication, history, and English. One student assistant from the Institute for Human Communication also participated in the retreat.

Summary of Day 1

The initial activity of the retreat provided an opportunity for faculty to define information competency and then outline the information competency skills that a college graduate should have. We discussed, synthesized, and posted the small-group findings.

Developing a Working Definition

The working definition that our large group synthesized after much discussion is as follows:

> **Information competency is the ability to identify
> a question/problem; access sources needed to answer,
> address, or solve the question/problem; and
> synthesize and utilize the information gathered,
> for the purpose of ethical decision making.**

The group then outlined the following skills as those necessary for an information-competent university graduate:

Ability to

- Determine types of information needed

- Know where to begin looking for information

- Understand and assume that others before you have pondered this topic and deserve respectful attention and credit

- Understand that information is value-laden and biased

- Understand that different types of information will transform the original question and ultimately put a new spin on the research requirements

- Know that specific information sources and research methodologies relate to specific disciplines

- Possess comprehension, analysis, evaluation, interpretation, and decision-making skills

- Understand that interpretation is intended for an audience

- Understand the demands of an intended audience

- Categorize types of retrieved information

- Understand the role of the researcher as an active participant in an ongoing conversation

- Understand that knowledge is context-bound

- Know when retrieved information is relevant to the research question

- Make a decision based on the available information

- Access and evaluate public information sources such as radio, television, people, newspapers, phone books

- Locate alternative sources of information and understand the purpose of such alternatives

- Conduct research without plagiarizing

- Publish information in the most relevant forms

Comparing Definitions, Standards, and Guidelines

In the next activity, the faculty began to think about the development of its own set of information competencies in alignment with existing sets previously developed by other organizations. In an effort not to reinvent the wheel, we asked the retreat participants to compare the HCOM large-group working definition and outline of information competency skills with the ACRL standards and with the work done by librarian Gabriela Sonntag and professor Renée Curry at our sister CSU campus in San Marcos, which had developed information competency assignment goals for their general education curriculum.

The purpose of this comparison was to introduce the HCOM faculty to the standards, attributes, and goals with which we were trying to align, as well as to demonstrate the various ways in which organizations assert unique approaches to information competency education based on particular institutional, divisional, or disciplinary visions. In small groups, faculty actively compared their definition with the ACRL and San Marcos standards and then began to note ways in which our major curriculum aligned with these standards and also furthered them in relation to our own vision.

Revisiting Lower-Division Information Competency at CSUMB

As a way of providing a foundation for our work on the human communication major, we took time during the retreat to refresh faculty memories regarding the CSUMB lower-division university learning requirement (ULR) in technology and information. The purpose of reviewing this material was to ensure that faculty understood the introductory and general level at which information competency is incorporated in the general education curriculum. We wanted to be sure that faculty understood the need for information competency education in the major that both built upon and particularized the competencies introduced in the lower division. The information competencies delivered in the major need to provide depth and interdisciplinary specificity. But first the faculty needed to understand the strengths and limitations of the technology and information ULR at CSUMB.

We have thirteen ULRs at CSUMB, one of which is a technology and information ULR. While achieving the technology and information ULR at the lower-division level, each student attains an introductory competence in nine learning outcomes:

- Using accepted word processing techniques to produce a well-designed and aesthetically pleasing formal document

- Using standard spreadsheet features to produce a representation and analysis of numerical data

- Identifying and refining a topic and formulating a research question related to that topic

- Describing and categorizing the basic types of information resources available in a variety of formats

- Locating, retrieving, and evaluating information relevant to the research question

- Organizing research findings to communicate conclusions and ideas

- Creating an electronic document that discusses a single subject or conveys a message

- Creating an original digital image

- Analyzing and responding to an ethical issue related to computers and use of information using a variety of sources

One of the main reasons we applied for the CSU information competency grant was that although our students do achieve basic competency in technology and information through the CSUMB ULR system, the Institute for Human Communication wanted to further students' learning by infusing information competencies into courses in the major. The upper-division coursework in human communication amplifies the skills attained in the lower division by focusing on disciplinary and interdisciplinary information competencies. We believe that alignment of these competencies with the learning that occurs in the major provides a depth of understanding of research skills that enhances the breadth of knowledge achieved in the technology and information ULR.

As an activity to begin the large-group discussion of the technology and information ULR, we brainstormed and charted all of the skills that HCOM faculty thought should be achieved in the technology and information ULR course. Not surprisingly, we all quickly came to validate the notion that one course, Technological Tools, cannot possibly fulfill all of students' information competency needs.

Developing Information Competency Assignments in the Major

Having thoroughly reviewed the technology and information ULR and the Technological Tools course, HCOM faculty felt quite certain about the skills that students entering the major did and did not have. The next step was to discuss infusion of information competency instruction into the major courses. Beginning this process required recognizing that a number of years ago, our institute had, in fact, had a set of criteria for assessing the information competence of our majors. We reviewed these previous assessment criteria, the San Marcos assessment criteria, and the University of California, Berkeley, Web site "Effective Assignments Using Library Resources" (University of California, Berkeley, Library, 2002), using them as a springboard for discussion of how to develop assignments in the major that focus on information competence. A commitment throughout the retreat was that whenever we could easily use other good work already done in our own university system or elsewhere, we would not reinvent the wheel. We did not want to create more work for ourselves or for the students.

We began this part of the work with a small-group critique of an assignment developed by CSUMB librarians. The assignment highlighted a number of difficult issues often seen by librarians in faculty wording of assignments. With good humor and wise scrutiny, the HCOM faculty discerned a number of difficult articulations that they themselves often employed in their own assignments. This activity provided a terrific way for faculty and librarians to verify with one another that we have similar goals and that, most of all, we need a common language in which to work with our students.

As a way of culminating the first day of the retreat and segueing into the second day, which addressed the major learning outcomes in HCOM, we had small groups of faculty develop an assignment that would ask students to research military conscription and its potential for reinstitution in light of the events of September 11, 2001. The faculty worked together to write a comprehensive research assignment that included

- A clear, concise description of assignment guidelines

- A requirement that students check in with the professor near the beginning of making discoveries and periodically thereafter

- Guidelines for finding and selecting quality sources

- A clear sense of the research methodology to be used

- Detailed options regarding the final research product

- A precise mode of assessment

At the end of the day, we all shared and critiqued the group assignments vis-à-vis the documents, standards, and criteria we had been studying all day.

The achievements of Day 1 included a deepened understanding of information competency standards, an awareness of the depth of information competency skills being delivered in the ULRs, an introduction to the goals and parameters of the grant initiative, and an experience of the collaboration necessary to infuse information competencies into the major.

Summary of Day 2

We began Day 2 of the Human Communication Information Competence Retreat with a large-group brainstorming session on the professional struggles we each have had in relationship to our students' lack of information competency skills. We used this session as a way to vent our frustrations and also as a way to look at the exact nature of the challenge we faced. Through this activity, we realized that the students actually do have quite a few skills on which we can build when they arrive at the major; however, the attributes and skills of information competency that we need to teach in HCOM are the standard information competency skills, along with the following particular interdisciplinary and affective approaches to research and creative inquiry:

Students will

- Develop and practice an understanding of the patience needed during the information acquisition phase

- Reflect upon the disciplinary limitations of their acquisitions and determine how to explore interdisciplinary possibilities

- Think about their acquired information in terms of its relationship to an ongoing disciplinary or interdisciplinary conversation, and integrate their own ideas smoothly into this conversation

- Compel themselves to continue their research through the moments when they discover material "too difficult" to understand

- Learn and practice how to acknowledge, respect, and cooperatively disagree with expertise in a field

- Learn how to abide frustration throughout the research process

- Experience intellectual joy

- Develop a scholarly or creative voice

- Incorporate their own experience effectively and appropriately into research

Aligning Major Learning Outcomes with the Information Competencies

The second activity of the day required that we begin thinking about how to align our outcomes-based curricular structure with the information competencies. In the Institute for Human Communication, we have major learning outcomes (MLOs). We require every major to complete successfully two core courses and three additional courses in a depth concentration, in addition to all of the following MLOs:

- *HCOM MLO 1, critical communication skills:* ability to communicate critically and empathically in both oral and written contexts, including reading, writing, listening, and speaking

- *HCOM MLO 2, research skills:* ability to acquire, evaluate, interpret, synthesize, apply, document, and present knowledge gained through diverse and appropriate methods of inquiry in the context of an analysis of an issue, question, or problem

- *HCOM MLO 3, relational communication skills:* ability to interact ethically and effectively in interpersonal and group communication and decision-making processes

- *HCOM MLO 4, philosophical analysis:* ability to understand why and how beliefs, values, assumptions, and communication practices interact to shape ways of being and knowing

- *HCOM MLO 5, critical cultural analysis:* ability to investigate and explain relationships among cultural ideologies and sociohistorical experiences, interests, identities, and actions of specific cultural groups

- *HCOM MLO 6, comparative literary analysis:* ability to appreciate and analyze literature in a social, historical, and cultural context; ability to compare and contrast literatures of at least three different cultural traditions, including non-Eurocentric traditions

- *HCOM MLO 7, historical analysis:* ability to actively engage our complex multicultural pasts by integrating historical understanding with historical thinking skills

- *HCOM MLO 8, creative writing and social action:* ability to acquire basic competency in creative writing; ability to apply this skill to the production and presentation of an art project that actively responds to a public issue; ability to sustain the creative process throughout a given project, taking it to completion

Each of the MLOs has well-articulated, published criteria for assessment; course-based and independent assessment-based pathways; and a set of assessment standards.

The Case of MLO 2, Research Skills

We began our alignment activities with MLO 2, research skills, because this was the learning outcome within which we had structured our information competency skills to date. There had been a number of problems with this approach that we had wanted to address for a long time. Thus, we divided into small groups to answer the following questions:

- To what degree is MLO 2, research skills, the place to concentrate our information competency efforts? We could actually teach and practice all of the information competencies in a course geared toward achieving MLO 2.

- To what extent do we want to infuse information competencies throughout the MLOs and the curriculum?

- Do we want to use a combination of thorough teaching of MLO 2 and infusion throughout the curriculum?

The result of this small-group activity and the ensuing discussion was extremely important to the curriculum. We decided to rework and redesign completely our HCOM 300 course—a proseminar that is an introduction to the major—to include thorough teaching of all the information competencies. Because the information competency grant provided us the necessary time to think about redesigning this course, we now have a proseminar with content that centers on the question, "What is an interdisciplinary degree in the humanities?" This course is now also infused with an introduction to information and technology competencies as they pertain to the interdisciplinary humanities.

Having made this enormous decision about MLO 2 and the HCOM 300 proseminar, we then moved on to an analysis of the infusion process and the other major learning outcomes.

Relevance of the Information Competencies
to the Human Communication Major

We reviewed CSU San Marcos's information competency checklist (shown in the Appendix at the end of this chapter) to see whether it included all of the information competencies that we discerned as important to our major. The CSU San Marcos (CSUSM) checklist specified the information competencies necessary to the CSUSM general education program. We began with this existing checklist because we did not want to reinvent the wheel. But we conducted a thorough review of the checklist because we wanted to modify the existing material so that it met our particular curricular needs. In a large group, we decided that we would keep all eight of the San Marcos competencies but that we would surely be adding our own as we continued our work. Immediately, we saw the need for the following two competencies:

- Does the assignment ask/encourage students to express and critique the feelings, values, and assumptions they have regarding the research question, issue, or problem? (This articulation became our competency #2.)

- Does the assignment ask/encourage students to interpret or creatively apply the retrieved material from a variety of perspectives? (This articulation became our competency #5.)

The articulation of these two competencies gave us a total of ten competencies with which to begin our discussion. (By the end of our yearlong process, we would have fourteen HCOM information competencies.)

We then divided into MLO-based small work groups. Each faculty member who taught a course that addressed one of the MLOs other than MLO 2 gathered in a group. Thus, we had an MLO 1 group, an MLO 3 group, and so on. The facilitators disseminated the CSU San Marcos information competency checklist and asked the MLO groups to name the competencies that were most naturally and already achieved in their MLO courses. Our purpose here was to encourage the faculty to understand that the information competency alignment with our major learning outcomes was a natural one and that we were not requesting more work of them. We simply needed more articulation of the information competencies that are being achieved in our courses.

After the small groups worked together to discern and articulate the alignment, we reported to the large group, and the facilitators recorded the exact information competencies that were being achieved in each of the MLOs. We recorded this information so that we would have a record of the alignment and so that we could use the information during our MLO case study sessions, which would occur as the second part of the grant work took place.

At the end of the second day of the retreat, we introduced the faculty to the purpose of the upcoming case studies. Each of the MLO groups would become a case study group. We would have two meetings each month to align the syllabi of the MLO courses with the information competencies decided upon at this retreat. We would also have a special case study regarding MLO 2 and the HCOM 300 proseminar, to redesign the course and align it with the information competencies.

The Case Studies

From January through May 2002, during the case study portion of the information competency grant, each of the MLO groups became a case study group. Two to four faculty members constituted each case study group, and each group worked together for two days. The goal of the case study sessions was to align the syllabi of the MLO courses with the information competencies decided upon at the September information competency retreat. We also had a special semester-long case study group on MLO 2 and the HCOM 300 proseminar, to redesign the course and align it with the information competencies.

Planning the Case Studies

In January, the grant recipients met twice to plan the case study work days. We decided to begin with MLO 2, since we actually had to redesign a course to accommodate the changes suggested at the retreat. During the planning sessions for the MLO 2 case study, we worked on the outcomes that we hoped to achieve:

- Develop a sound curricular method for working on *all* of the information competencies in HCOM 300 as well as an articulation of the alignment between the information competencies and MLO 2 in the HCOM 300 course assignments

- Work with the Technology and Information University Learning Requirement Committee to align the technology outcomes of this course with the technology and information ULR

- Redesign the course so that the content addresses becoming information competent in an interdisciplinary humanities major

- Retain the attributes of the course that advise students about the major's MLOs, concentrations, individual learning plan deadlines, capstone requirements, and so on

The planning sessions for the other case studies involved designing a case study format. The format we decided on was the following:

- Faculty will bring their MLO course syllabi (enough copies for the whole group) to the case study meeting

- Faculty will bring a set of assignments related to the syllabi and achievement of the MLO

- Facilitators Renée Curry and Pam Baker will bring the retreat's preliminary alignment suggestions as a springboard for discussion on aligning MLOs and information competencies

- Facilitators will bring the information competency checklist

- Facilitators will begin the process by having the case study group do the following:

  - Analyze the checklist for any needed revisions or additions
  - Study the preliminary alignment suggestions for precision and accuracy of alignment
  - Read through the syllabus for language that might be revised to better articulate the alignment between the major learning outcomes and the information competencies
  - Revise the assignments to better articulate the information competencies and to better demonstrate the information competencies
  - Verify that the in-class assessment for the MLO also assesses the level of information competency

The participants in each case study session included the entire full-time tenure-track faculty, quite a few of the part-time faculty, an instructional technologist, two faculty librarians, and a student assistant. Faculty from the following disciplinary and interdisciplinary units participated in the case studies of their syllabi: Spanish Literature and New Media, History, Ethnic American Literatures,

Women's Studies, Film Studies, Philosophy, Communication, Ethics, Cultural Studies, Chicana/Chicano and Latina/Latino Studies, Creative Writing, and English.

Implementing the Case Studies

Although we actually conducted eight case studies, in this chapter, we will highlight two unique cases.

Case Study of MLO 2, Research Analysis

As the curriculum in human communication was originally conceived, the outcomes for MLO 2, research analysis, typically were attained within the history or literature courses that required research papers. Over the years, this situation proved more and more difficult for two reasons: (1) each of the history and literature courses were also responsible for delivering assessment opportunities in historical analysis and comparative literary analysis; and 2) many students did not take these courses early in their careers, which meant that they were lacking significant research analysis skills while participating in their major curriculum. By teaching within an outcomes-based curriculum, we came to realize the untenability of trying to attain two major learning outcomes within one course and the significant disadvantages associated with teaching research skills in a concurrent fashion rather than using a skill-building infusion method. Thus the opportunity to study our MLO 2 research analysis courses with the support of the grant enabled us to amend two difficulties that we had already been experiencing.

In the case study, we discussed the possibility of moving MLO 2 out of the literature and history courses and into the HCOM 300 proseminar course. All students coming into the HCOM major must take the HCOM 300 proseminar; thus, by transferring MLO 2 to this introductory course, we would ensure that all new students would attain at least an introductory capability in the research skills necessary to participate in our interdisciplinary humanities program.

While contemplating this curricular move, we analyzed an allied difficulty that had been plaguing the proseminar for some time. Student evaluations had pegged this course as one lacking in content. It is true that we used the course to introduce the students to outcomes-based learning, independent learning plans, selection of concentrations, and development of capstone projects, but we had not had the time to revisit the course in a thorough and reflective manner in regard to the content issue. After spending some time discussing the knowledge we had attained at the information competency retreat, we decided that the HCOM proseminar was most likely lacking in linking content. We had thought that the students understood what it meant to be in an interdisciplinary program but had never really taught them what an interdisciplinary program was. Therefore, we redesigned the entire course to include historical content on the advent of interdisciplinary studies, the practice of interdisciplinary studies, and a bit of interdisciplinary theory. As well, we designed learning activities that provided students with opportunities to apply their newly acquired interdisciplinary knowledge.

Once we had redesigned the content curriculum, we developed a content syllabus and then set about developing activities that would pertain to all fourteen of the HCOM information competencies on the checklist shown in Exhibit 4.1. The case study group for MLO 2, research analysis, took the entire semester to develop activities pertinent to the information competencies.

MLO 2 and the University Learning Requirement in Technology

In addition to these information competency incorporation activities, the MLO 2 case study group took on the additional task of obtaining approval from the Technology and Information University Learning Requirement Committee for the HCOM 300 course as one in which students could attain their university learning requirement in technology. The ULR program at CSUMB is comparable to the general education programs at most universities. We

Exhibit 4.1. HCOM Information Competency Checklist

Does the assignment ask/encourage students to . . .

_____ 1. articulate a research question, creative investigation, issue, or problem based in the humanities?

_____ 2. express and critique the feelings, values, and assumptions they have regarding the research question or creative investigation?

_____ 3. make multiple and different determinations about the types of disciplinary and interdisciplinary sources necessary to complete the research?

_____ 4. conduct research through electronic and book-based data retrieval systems?

_____ 5. interpret or creatively apply the retrieved material from a variety of perspectives?

_____ 6. make selections from, integrate, and synthesize information retrieved in their search?

_____ 7. analyze and evaluate the credibility of the information retrieved?

_____ 8. use computer literacy skills and technology platforms related to the humanities?

_____ 9. demonstrate an understanding of fair use of copyrighted material and intellectual property?

_____10. develop long-term, adaptable, cross-disciplinary research and/or creative application skills?

_____11. communicate research findings and/or creative production in an effective, aesthetic, and ethical manner?

_____12. create or construct new thought, imagery (textual and/or visual), or theory from the synthesis of sources?

_____13. validate understanding through collaboration with other people?

_____14. respond actively to a social justice issue?

Source: Developed by Renée R. Curry and Gabriela Sonntag, California State University San Marcos, 1999. Revised by the Institute for Human Communication, California State University Monterey Bay, 2001–2002.

especially wanted our transfer HCOM majors to be able to attain their upper-division technology ULR in the HCOM 300 proseminar. The students who came to the HCOM proseminar through our own four-year curriculum would be required to meet both the lower-division technology ULR and the upper-division technology component of our own program.

One rationale for attempting to obtain the technology and information ULR approval was that many of our humanities faculty had become involved with both media analysis and new media dissemination of their research. *New media* is a term that encompasses much of the sophisticated computer technology now available, including streaming audio, streaming video, DVD recordings, highly interactive user interfaces, and virtual reality environments, among others. Much of the literature on the future of the humanities emphasizes the impact of new media in the classroom. Three of our faculty are deeply involved with the national Visible Knowledge Project, based at Georgetown University (Visible Knowledge Project, 2002), and many of our other faculty have been incorporating new media in their courses. Our curriculum thus requires that students be equipped not only to analyze media but also to create research projects and disseminate research findings with new media. To help our students succeed in the major, we had to develop the HCOM proseminar so that it provided ample opportunities for students to learn how to work with spreadsheets, analyze and create digitized representations, deliver PowerPoint presentations, and create digital videos for the purpose of disseminating research in the humanities.

To obtain approval from the Technology and Information University Learning Requirement Committee for our course, we had to work with the committee and an instructional technologist to develop and revise our curricular activities. The committee was rigorous in its standards, and we went through numerous revisions. Without the help of the grant, we would not have been able to support the faculty who worked so diligently on this case, nor would we have been able to hire the instructional technologist who both enabled us to design coursework activities suitable for our humanities students and trained us in the pedagogies necessary to teach students how best to work with new media.

The result of two semesters of work is that we now have technology ULR approval for our HCOM 300 proseminar course, and students who complete the course will receive an introduction to information competencies that includes new media and is tailored to the human communication major. In subsequent courses such as Social Impact of the Mass Media; Media Ethics; Latina Life Stories; Introduction to Creative Writing; Race, Colonialism, and Film; Oral History and Community Memory; Multicultural History in the New Media Classroom; and Media Production Lab, students analyze news media, create digital stories, critique ideologies of feature films, author and design e-zines, digitize oral histories for community projects, create digital histories, and produce on-line magazines. These are some of the activities most relevant to the new humanities.

As revised, the HCOM 300 proseminar now introduces all of the research skills, information competencies, and technological competencies necessary in our interdisciplinary humanities curriculum. Subsequent courses then broaden and deepen student understanding and application of the information competencies.

Case Study of MLO 8, Creative Writing and Social Action

The case study for MLO 8 was the last case study we conducted. As in the other case studies, the faculty brought syllabi to align with the information competencies. And, as was true with all of the other case studies, faculty discovered that they had indeed been providing students with numerous opportunities to attain certain of the information competencies but that neither the activities nor the syllabi clearly articulated the competencies. Like the faculty in the other case studies, the MLO 8 group decided on language that could be incorporated into their assignments.

The MLO 8 case study group veered away from the rest of the groups, however, in the language they decided to use to articulate their competencies. Part of the unique challenge faced by the creative writing and social action case study group was that the language of the ACRL standards, the CSU standards, and our own adapted HCOM information competencies relied heavily on traditional research language that relegated creative investigation to the periphery. For instance, this case study group pointed out that language asking whether an assignment "articulates a research question, issue, or problem" does not address the types of creative inquiry undertaken by poets, fiction writers, or screenwriters. The MLO 8 group encouraged the faculty to revise the language of the HCOM information competency checklist as an articulation of the fact that creative investigation is a research skill important to the humanities, one that we want each of our graduates to attain.

Of the fourteen points approved or developed by our faculty, the MLO 8 study group is responsible for language changes in eight of them (shown in bold on Exhibit 4.2).

Clearly, the impact of the MLO 8 case study group on the articulation of the information competencies attained in our major was remarkable. Once again, we have to say that without the support of the grant, which enabled us to have needed time together, the collaborative underpinnings of our curriculum would not have been expressed in the way that we have now articulated them.

Alignment of Information Competencies with Major Learning Outcomes

As of September 2002, every syllabus distributed to HCOM majors at CSUMB articulates the information competencies attained in the course. The competencies attained in each course are aligned with the eight major learning outcomes of the curriculum. They are articulated in a standard, yet flexible way, to accommodate differences in language used by the various disciplines and interdisciplinary units that make up our curriculum. The syllabus language is shown in Exhibit 4.3.

Exhibit 4.2. HCOM Information Competency Checklist, Showing Language Changes Requested by the MLO 8 Case Study Group

Does the assignment ask/encourage students to . . .

_____ 1. articulate a research question, **creative investigation,** issue, or problem based in the humanities?

_____ 2. express and critique the feelings, values, and assumptions they have regarding the research question **or creative investigation?**

_____ 3. make multiple and different determinations about the types of disciplinary and interdisciplinary sources necessary to complete the research?

_____ 4. conduct research through electronic and book-based data retrieval systems?

_____ 5. interpret **or creatively apply** the retrieved material from a variety of perspectives?

_____ 6. make selections from, integrate, and synthesize information retrieved in their search?

_____ 7. analyze and evaluate the credibility of the information retrieved?

_____ 8. use computer literacy skills and technology platforms related to the humanities?

_____ 9. demonstrate an understanding of fair use of copyrighted material and intellectual property?

_____10. develop long-term, adaptable, cross-disciplinary research **and/or creative application skills?**

_____11. communicate research findings **and/or creative production** in an effective, **aesthetic,** and ethical manner?

_____12. **create or construct new thought, imagery (textual and/or visual),** or theory from the synthesis of sources?

_____13. **validate understanding through collaboration with other people?**

_____14. **respond actively to a social justice issue?**

Source: Developed by Renée R. Curry and Gabriela Sonntag, California State University San Marcos, 1999. Revised by the Institute for Human Communication, California State University Monterey Bay, 2001–2002.

**Exhibit 4.3. HCOM Major Learning Outcomes and
the Association of College and Research Libraries
Information Competence Standards in Higher Education**

Alignment Document
August 2002

MLO 1, Critical Communication Skills
    In alignment with the Association of College and Research Libraries
standards, HCOM courses meeting MLO 1, critical communication
skills, will assess students' information competence through their
abilities to

- Articulate a research question, creative investigation, issue, or
  problem based in the humanities
- Express and critique the feelings, values, and assumptions they
  have regarding the research question or creative investigation
- Make multiple and different determinations about the types of
  disciplinary and interdisciplinary sources necessary to complete
  the research
- Interpret or creatively apply the retrieved material from a variety
  of perspectives
- Make selections from, integrate, and synthesize information
  retrieved in their search
- Analyze and evaluate the credibility of the information retrieved

    MLO 1 courses will focus on all of the above information
competencies, with a special emphasis on making determinations about
sources and analyzing credibility.

MLO 2, Research Skills
    In alignment with the Association of College and Research Libraries
standards, HCOM courses meeting MLO 2, research skills, will assess
students' information competence through their abilities to

- Articulate a research question, creative investigation, issue, or
  problem based in the humanities
- Express and critique the feelings, values, and assumptions they
  have regarding the research question or creative investigation

Exhibit 4.3. HCOM Major Learning Outcomes and the Association of College and Research Libraries Information Competence Standards in Higher Education, *continued*

- Make multiple and different determinations about the types of disciplinary and interdisciplinary sources necessary to complete the research
- Conduct research through electronic and book-based data retrieval systems
- Interpret or creatively apply the retrieved material from a variety of perspectives
- Make selections from, integrate, and synthesize information retrieved in their search
- Analyze and evaluate the credibility of the information retrieved
- Use computer literacy skills and technology platforms related to the humanities
- Demonstrate an understanding of fair use of copyrighted material and intellectual property
- Develop long-term, adaptable, cross-disciplinary research and/or creative application skills
- Communicate research findings and/or creative production in an effective, aesthetic, and ethical manner
- Create or construct new thought, imagery, or theory from the synthesis of sources
- Validate understanding through collaboration with other people
- Respond actively to a social justice issue

MLO 2 courses will focus on all of the above information competencies.

MLO 3, Relational Communication Skills

In alignment with the Association of College and Research Libraries standards, HCOM courses meeting MLO 3, relational communication skills, will assess students' information competence through their abilities to

- Express and critique the feelings, values, and assumptions they have regarding the research question or creative investigation

- Interpret or creatively apply the retrieved material from a variety of perspectives

MLO 3 courses will emphasize the expression and critique of feelings, values, and assumptions.

MLO 4, *Philosophical Analysis*

In alignment with the Association of College and Research Libraries standards, HCOM courses meeting MLO 4, philosophical analysis, will assess students' information competence through their abilities to

- Express and critique the feelings, values, and assumptions they have regarding the research question or creative investigation
- Interpret or creatively apply the retrieved material from a variety of perspectives

MLO 4 courses will emphasize the expression and critique of feelings, values, and assumptions.

MLO 5, *Critical Cultural Analysis*

In alignment with the Association of College and Research Libraries standards, HCOM courses meeting MLO 5, critical cultural analysis, will assess students' information competence through their abilities to

- Express and critique the feelings, values, and assumptions they have regarding the research question or creative investigation
- Make multiple and different determinations about the types of disciplinary and interdisciplinary sources necessary to complete the research
- Interpret or creatively apply the retrieved material from a variety of perspectives
- Develop long-term, adaptable, cross-disciplinary research and/or creative application skills

MLO 5 courses will emphasize the determination of sources, interpretation of perspectives, and long-term adaptability.

MLO 6, *Comparative Literary Analysis*

In alignment with the Association of College and Research Libraries standards, HCOM courses meeting MLO 6, comparative literary

**Exhibit 4.3. HCOM Major Learning Outcomes and
the Association of College and Research Libraries
Information Competence Standards in Higher Education,** *continued*

analysis, will assess students' information competence through their abilities to

- Articulate a research question, creative investigation, issue, or problem based in the humanities
- Express and critique the feelings, values, and assumptions they have regarding the research question or creative investigation
- Interpret or creatively apply the retrieved material from a variety of perspectives
- Use computer literacy skills and technology platforms related to the humanities
- Demonstrate an understanding of fair use of copyrighted material and intellectual property

MLO 6 courses will emphasize computer literacy and understanding of intellectual property.

MLO 7, Historical Analysis

In alignment with the Association of College and Research Libraries standards, HCOM courses meeting MLO 7, historical analysis, will assess students' information competence through their abilities to

- Articulate a research question, creative investigation, issue, or problem based in the humanities
- Make multiple and different determinations about the types of disciplinary and interdisciplinary sources necessary to complete the research
- Conduct research through electronic and book-based data retrieval systems
- Make selections from, integrate, and synthesize information retrieved in their search
- Analyze and evaluate the credibility of the information retrieved

MLO 7 courses will emphasize the determination of sources, retrieval systems, integration and synthesis, and evaluation of credibility.

MLO 8, Creative Writing and Social Action

In alignment with the Association of College and Research Libraries standards, HCOM courses meeting MLO 8, creative writing and social action, will assess students' information competence through their abilities to

- Articulate a creative inquiry, research question, issue, or problem based in the humanities
- Express and critique the feelings, values, and assumptions they have regarding the creative investigation or research question
- Creatively apply or interpret the retrieved material from a variety of perspectives
- Develop long-term, adaptable, cross-disciplinary research and/or creative application skills
- Communicate their creative production and/or research findings in an effective, aesthetic, and ethical manner
- Create or construct new thought, imagery (textual and/or visual), or theory from the synthesis of sources
- Validate understanding through collaboration with other people
- Respond actively to a social justice issue

MLO 8 courses will emphasize the creative production, expression, and critique of feelings; creation of new thought and imagery (textual and visual); and response to a social justice issue.

Recommendations

During the course of our project, we hoped to gain insight into how we could enrich our students' learning experiences through careful integration and articulation of information competence learning outcomes. We did not anticipate but were delighted with the deeper understanding we gained in one another's areas of expertise, discovering how this too would benefit our students, as well as our own endeavors.

The following recommendations are based on the first phase of our successful yearlong project; they stress the planning process, support we had in place, and lessons learned from mutual endeavor.

Funding

Acquiring adequate funding was crucial for a project of this scope and size. It is important to acknowledge the expertise and commitment of the participants and to compensate them as generously as possible. As members of the California State University, we were fortunate to be part of the largest state university system in the country, one with a well-established and supportive information competence initiative. There have been many opportunities for the campuses to fund both small and large projects, and we were able to secure a generous grant that enabled us to plan and carry out our ambitious ideas.

The most important recommendation we can make is to designate someone who actively seeks out initiatives or other grant possibilities that exist at your own institution. Many such funding sources remain invisible to the average librarian or faculty member. Your campus faculty development center and the grants and contracts office at your local campus or statewide institution are good places to start, but be creative in seeking out other sources of funding.

Administrative Support

Another crucial factor in the success of a project is strong ideological and financial support from administrators who have a holistic vision of the importance of your project and how it benefits the department and the campus as a whole. We were fortunate to have this support on a variety of levels.

Since its inception in 1995, CSU Monterey Bay has had a strong campus commitment to an information literacy requirement. In our case, the director of the Institute for Human Communication initiated the project, which eliminated the need to justify the importance of information competency at the department level. We also had the complete support of the library director (and the support and interest of the interim dean of the arts and humanities center). The library director participated as a planner and facilitator of the two-day retreat, and he also participated in several of the case studies. The interim dean participated in one day of the retreat.

Identifying Partners

Needless to say, a project like ours works only when faculty and librarians have a highly collaborative relationship. We needed library faculty and discipline faculty as well as instructional technologists, all working as partners to envision goals, establish outcomes, and accomplish the actual work of articulating and integrating information competency outcomes into the human communication major.

No member of an academic institution should have to start from scratch. Make use of your existing library-discipline partnerships and build on them. At CSU Monterey Bay, all librarians provide course-related or course-integrated instruction to many departments across campus. Three of the librarians already had long-standing relationships with the human communication faculty—team teaching, previous grant work, and, in the case of the library instruction coordinator, even providing faculty development sessions on information competence content and pedagogy. We built on the trust that had already been developed in these relationships to forge a highly collaborative working group.

What We Have Learned

After developing the grant proposal, implementing the two-day retreat to infuse information competencies into the Institute's major learning outcomes, and reflecting on the process, we have learned a number of lessons worth sharing.

Don't Reinvent the Wheel!

As we have stated throughout this chapter, use your knowledge of campus goals and priorities for information literacy to begin discussions with potential partners. Also make use of your knowledge regarding the particular curricular visions of your library or partnering departments to collaborate on an attainable goal. Do not be afraid to expand the relationships you have already nurtured across departments or with the library.

Don't forget that existing information competency standards can be used as your beginning point. A crucial step in our process was adapting these standards to our local curricular vision. By all means, modify existing standards to reflect your local academic culture.

Common Ground

From the beginning of the project, we stressed to all participants that no matter what differences might arise in our work together, our common ground was the students. At the retreat and throughout the case studies, we frequently articulated our mutual goal as "helping our students to develop lifelong information literacy skills." Even though approaches and vocabulary differed among faculty and librarians many times throughout our year together, we always agreed ultimately that the learning experiences of the students should be as clear and beneficial as possible.

Different Vocabularies

Although it seems obvious to us now, we came to realize that the human communication faculty had their own knowledge of information literacy issues and that their vocabulary was quite different from that of the ACRL standards familiar to librarians. By permitting open, creative, and empathic discussion to occur and by keeping the needs of the students in mind, the library faculty were always able to agree on language suitable for expressing the competencies and accommodating the interdisciplinary nature of the degree program. Likewise, the interdisciplinary faculty learned that in order for course assignments to be shared in mutual endeavor with library faculty, some standardized language has to be used. When faculty actively attend to the multiple audiences and purposes of vocabulary used in course assignments, we can enrich the information competency standards and actualize them as usable and effective student learning skills.

Future Assessment

We spent a great deal of time this past year carefully tailoring the information competencies in our curriculum to the departmental vision of interdisciplinarity. We diligently aligned information competencies with major learning outcomes, reworked syllabi, and clarified the information competency language used in course assignments. Through the work with each syllabus in the case studies, it became clear that we would only be able to assess the competencies if we could clearly and concisely articulate them.

Because we are an outcomes-based educational institution, in addition to more formal assessment (tests, portfolios, final projects), our faculty already employs several types of carefully articulated in-class assessments based on pre-established and published criteria for meeting the major learning outcomes. To ensure that our students can demonstrate our stated information competence outcomes, the third and final part of our project will be to develop appropriate assessment instruments.

Broadening Relationships

Over the course of the year, the participants also recognized that we had gained some valuable insight on a level deeper than that of curriculum development. The close working relationship between the library instruction coordinator and the human communication faculty opened a network of mutual trust and communication that extended beyond the grant work; we created new access points for information sharing in related areas. For example, the library instruction coordinator is also chair of the CSUMB university learning requirement for technology and information competence. When, as a result of the Information Competence Grant Initiative, the Institute for Human Communication decided to restructure their HCOM 300 proseminar, the HCOM representative was able to trust the ULR chair and the ULR committee's request for revisions. Too often, because faculty, librarians, and administrators do not have trusting relationships across disciplinary groups and divisions, we are reluctant to hear committee suggestions as constructive opportunities to better our programs. Collaborative projects such as the grant initiative serve to build the trust necessary to develop cooperative academic environments.

Taking Risks

Many of the grant participants felt an element of risk in letting go of their own and others' work. As our work proceeded, we deemed it worth taking the risk in order to gain deeper understandings of one another's work. The potential for clarifying and easing the way for our students to have effective learning experiences made every risk worthwhile.

Appendix

Information Competencies Activity/Assignment Checklist
General Education Programs
California State University San Marcos

_____ 1. Does assignment ask/encourage students to articulate a research question, issue or problem?

_____ 2. Does assignment ask/encourage students to make multiple and different determinations about the types of sources necessary to complete the research?

_____ 3. Does assignment ask/encourage students to conduct research through electronic and book-based data retrieval systems?

_____ 4. Does assignment ask/encourage students to make selections from, integrate, and synthesize information retrieved in their search?

_____ 5. Does assignment ask/encourage students to analyze and evaluate the credibility of the information retrieved?

_____ 6. Does assignment ask/encourage students to utilize computer literacy skills to communicate their research discoveries?

_____ 7. Does assignment ask/encourage students to demonstrate an understanding of fair use of copyrighted material and intellectual property?

_____ 8. Does assignment ask/encourage students to develop long-term, adaptable, cross-disciplinary research skills?

Source: Developed by Gabriela Sonntag and Renée R. Curry, California State University San Marcos, 1998–1999.

References

American Library Association. "Presidential Committee on Information Literacy (Released on January 10, 1989, in Washington D.C.)" 1989. http://www.ala.org/acrl/nili/ilit1st.html. Accessed Oct. 25, 2002.

Association of College and Research Libraries. *Information Literacy Competency Standards for Higher Education*. Chicago: Association of College and Research Libraries, 2000. Also available at http://www.ala.org/Content/ NavigationMenu/ACRL/Standards_and_Guidelines/Information_ Literacy_Competency_Standards_for_Higher_Education.htm. Accessed Oct. 28, 2002.

Association of College and Research Libraries, Institute for Information Literacy. "Other Information Literacy Resources." 2002. http://staging. ala.org/ala/acrl/acrlissues/acr/infolit/acr/instinfolit/resources.htm. Accessed Jan. 14, 2002.

Atkins, Priscilla. "Information Literacy and the Arts: Be There—or Miss It!" *College and Research Libraries News*, Dec. 2001, 62(11), 1086–1088.

Baker, Pam, and Renée R. Curry. *Information Competency Grant Initiative*. Monterey: California State University Monterey Bay, 2002, p. 1.

Brown, Cecelia, and Lee R. Krumholz. "Integrating Information Literacy into the Science Curriculum." *College and Research Libraries*, Mar. 2002, 63(2), 111–123.

Bruce, Christine. "Information Literacy Programs and Research: An International Review." *Australian Library Journal*, 2000, 49(3), 209–218.

California Polytechnic State University. "IC in Specific Disciplines." In "CSU Information Competence Project." Updated Apr. 18, 2001. http://www. lib.calpoly.edu/infocomp/specific.html. Retrieved Oct. 27, 2002.

California State University. "Integration of Learning Outcomes." In "Information Competence Initiative." Updated Sept. 10, 2002. http://www. calstate.edu/LS/Outcomes.shtml. Retrieved Oct. 29, 2002.

California State University Fullerton. "Assessing Information Competence Across Disciplines." 1999. http://guides.library.fullerton.edu/infocomp/ CLRIT.htm#Abstract. Retrieved Oct. 27, 2002.

California State University Long Beach. "Information Competence in Philosophy." Updated June 12, 2002. http://csulb.edu/~philos/ information/. Retrieved Oct. 29, 2002. California State University Monterey Bay. *California State University Monterey Bay Catalog 2002–2003*. Vol. 7. Monterey: California State University Monterey Bay, Apr. 2002a.

California State University Monterey Bay. "California State University Monterey Bay On-Line Catalog 2002–2003." 2002b. http://csumb.edu. Retrieved Dec. 20, 2002.

California State University San Marcos. "Information Competence as a Student Learning Outcome: Developing Engaged Students in Business Disciplines." 2002. http://library.csusm.edu/departments/ilp/ilp_projects/buscomp/index.html. Retrieved Oct. 29, 2002.

Council of Australian University Librarians. *Information Literacy Standards*. 2001. http://www.caul.edu.au/caul-doc/InfoLit Standards2001.doc. Retrieved Oct. 30, 2002.

Curzon, Susan C. "CSU Information Competence Projects." In "Information Competence." Modified July 9, 2002. http://library.csun.edu/susan.curzon/infocmp.html#five. Retrieved Oct. 26, 2002.

Daugherty, Timothy K., and Elizabeth W. Carter. "Assessment of Outcome-Focused Library Instruction in Psychology." *Journal of Instructional Psychology*, Mar. 1997, *24*(1), 25–29.

Dorner, Jennifer L., and Susan E. Taylor. "Faculty-Librarian Collaboration for Nursing Information Literacy: A Tiered Approach." *Reference Services Review*, 2001, *29*(2), 132–140.

Gauss, Nancy Venditti, and William E. King. "Integrating Information Literacy into Freshman Composition: Beginning a Long and Beautiful Friendship." *Colorado Libraries*, Winter 1998, *24*(4), 17–20.

Humboldt State University. "Information Competency for History Majors." 2002. http://sorrelfp.humboldt.edu/ap23/infocomp/index.htm. Retrieved Oct. 29, 2002.

Moran, Joe. *Interdisciplinarity*. New York: Routledge, 2002. p. 15.

San Jose State University. "Information Competency in the Biology Curriculum." Updated Sept. 28, 2001. http://www.sjsu.edu/~cbhope/biology/infocomp/default.htm. Retrieved Oct. 28, 2002.

University of California, Berkeley, Library. "Effective Assignments Using Library Resources." Updated Aug. 14, 2002. http://www.lib.berkeley.edu/TeachingLib/assignments.html. Retrieved Jan. 14, 2002.

Visible Knowledge Project. *Visible Knowledge Project*. 2002. http://crossroads.georgetown.edu/vkp. Retrieved Jan. 14, 2003.

5

Meeting Information Literacy Needs in a Research Setting

Trudi E. Jacobson

Large research institutions face a variety of challenges when they endeavor to implement or enhance an information literacy program. Some of these challenges are unique to institutions of this type. This chapter will identify some of these factors, and look briefly at the ways in which several research institutions have addressed these factors. An in-depth analysis of the situation at the University at Albany follows. While this scenario is local to the University at Albany, we have learned a number of important things during our efforts that may be of use to faculty members, librarians, and administrators at other institutions. Although the University at Albany is a research institution, our efforts thus far have addressed the information literacy needs of undergraduates, just as many other institutions around the country are doing. However, information literacy initiatives are being recognized as necessary for graduate students as well.

Challenges of Information Literacy at Large Research Institutions

Implementing information literacy efforts at any type or size of school presents a number of hurdles. There are issues of buy-in by key players (faculty members, administrators, library administrators, and librarians), situating the program so that it is visible and effective, integrating information literacy with the general education program, and a host of other challenges that may be unique to a particular institution. Beyond these challenges, large research institutions face a number of others. These include the scalability of programs; professors and teaching assistants who are unaware of the benefits of information literacy; the status of librarians; and the decentralized libraries found on some large campuses.

At smaller or strictly undergraduate institutions, the emphasis may rest entirely on an undergraduate information literacy program. The general education program may be sufficiently focused that a natural venue for information literacy instruction can be easily identified. At larger institutions, there most likely will not be such a focus. Instead, information literacy must be diffused throughout a variety of programs if it is to reach a large number of students, or it must reach thousands of students in a single format. On smaller campuses, new initiatives such as information literacy can be discussed in meetings that are likely to reach a large proportion of faculty members. On large campuses, such meeting opportunities do not exist. In addition, research institutions rely not only on faculty members but also teaching assistants. This makes efforts to spread the word about information literacy even more difficult. The third special challenge is the status of librarians. At some schools, they have faculty or equivalent academic status. This smoothes the way for their interactions with discipline faculty members and also allows the option of their teaching credit-bearing information literacy courses. On campuses where librarians do not have faculty status, discipline faculty members may be less accustomed to working closely with librarians in settings such as faculty governance and curriculum development. On smaller campuses, librarian status may not have the repercussions it does at larger institutions, since librarians tend to work closely with discipline faculty members on a number of matters regardless of status. Last, it is easier to develop and implement an information literacy program when there is one library or, at most, several. When there are many librarians dispersed throughout a number of libraries, coordination becomes an important issue and may adversely affect implementation of a master information literacy program.

Information Literacy Initiatives at Large Research Institutions

Some research institutions had programs in place long before the use of the term *information literacy*. One example is Iowa State University, which began offering a course called "Library Use Instruction" in 1890. The course, Library 160, is now a half-credit course that all undergraduates must take. It has evolved from a lecture-based course to one that is mostly self-paced, with just one class meeting (http://www.lib.iastate.edu/class/lib160/about_lib160.html). It is recommended that students take it as early as possible in their undergraduate career. Librarians, who have faculty status, also offer course-related instruction at the request of discipline faculty members.

At Indiana University–Purdue University Indianapolis (IUPUI), where librarians have tenure-track academic status, a very different approach has been used. A dean (library)-to-dean (University College, where freshman learning communities are situated) initiative ensured that librarians would be included in instructional teams. These instructional teams are composed of a member of the teaching faculty, a librarian, a counselor, and a student mentor, who prepare or revise courses (http://www-lib.iupui.edu/itt/). Bill Orme, until recently IUPUI instructional teams' team leader and currently leader of the University College team, notes, "There has been a trend among academic librarians to develop 'information literacy' or 'critical thinking' courses. This approach contains an implicit assumption that these competencies exist as a separate part of the curriculum when, in fact, they need to be an integral part of the entire curriculum, regardless of the discipline involved" (Orme, 1999). In this model, the team approach ensures close cooperation between library and discipline faculty (and others). The model is flexible, and it can be used to integrate information literacy instruction into courses in a wide variety of areas. However, the program is so labor-intensive that it is not scalable. At present, it is used within freshman learning community courses, but there is a desire to maximize the impact of the instructional team approach by moving it from freshman to upper-division undergraduate courses and to rely more heavily on Web-based tutorials at the freshman level. The instructional team approach has been extremely beneficial in raising the stature of librarians on campus, because librarians work very closely with faculty members on instructional issues. IUPUI is a decentralized campus, where a variety of initiatives are occurring—for example, there are strong partnership efforts involving librarians with freshmen in the School of Science and involving faculty and librarians at the medical school (Bill Orme, personal communication, Sept. 24 and Sept. 27, 2002).

The University of California Los Angeles (UCLA) has thirteen different libraries, many of which provide information literacy instruction. However, UCLA librarians have just begun the new systemwide Information Literacy Initiative. The goal is "to help members of the UCLA community master conceptual and practical information literacy skills to enrich their educational, professional and personal lives, and enable them to become independent lifelong learners" (http://www.library.ucla.edu/infolit/about.html). UCLA librarians have formed five interest groups to address issues relating to information literacy, including collaborating, informing, measuring, outreach, and instructional development. These interest groups will be considering areas that are challenging to information literacy programs at research institutions, such as providing "mechanisms to further coordination, communication, and collaboration relating to information literacy activities and approaches in UCLA libraries," furthering "a sequenced approach to information literacy by facilitating communication and partnering among librarians and faculty," and increasing "campus awareness of information literacy issues and Initiative efforts" (http://www.library.ucla.edu/infolit/about.html).

The University of Washington has a number of initiatives related to information literacy. The UWired program, which addressed the use of information technology for pedagogical purposes, lives on in projects such as Catalyst® (http://catalyst.washington.edu/). Catalyst involves the local development of Web-based tools that focus on teaching, such as threaded discussions, easy Web page development for syllabi, on-line peer review of materials, and on-line portfolios. It also provides resources and support for the use of these tools. Although various pilot projects sponsored by UWired (for example, a course that was team taught by a librarian and an undergraduate peer instructor) were not scalable, the libraries continue to build on the collaborative relationships established at that time. For example, instructional collaborations initiated under UWired led to the development of an optional discipline-related, credit-bearing course, Information Research Strategies, taught by librarians and offered through the Information School. Recent sections have concentrated on history (Researching Victorian England), communications, and the environmental and natural sciences. Another information literacy program that builds upon the Catalyst model is the u*will* project (http://www.lib.washington.edu/uwill/index.html). This Web-based information literacy tutorial provides around-the-clock access from any computer, and was designed to address problems concerning the scalability and effectiveness of fifty-minute workshops. There have been pilot projects to customize the tutorial for a variety of large lecture courses, and the ultimate goal is to develop a database-driven Web application that will allow desktop access for librarians and faculty members to customize the tutorial to their own discipline (Anne Zald, personal communication, Sept. 30, Oct. 4, and Oct, 8, 2002).

Information Literacy at the University at Albany

The struggle to implement information literacy instruction at the University at Albany has been going on for a decade. Various meritorious initiatives have bloomed and faded without making much of an impact on campus. It has not been easy, but the university finally does have a general education information literacy requirement, which is already having a marked, positive effect on students' information literacy skills.

Background on the University at Albany

The University at Albany (hereafter called "Albany") is one of four university centers in the State University of New York (SUNY) system. In addition to the four university centers, there are thirteen university colleges, eight technology colleges, and thirty community colleges. SUNY is governed by a board of trustees.

Albany has approximately 12,000 undergraduate students, more than 5,300 graduate students, and more than 900 faculty members (595 full-time faculty). Campus plans call for an increase to 20,000 students. There are forty-seven librarians, who hold faculty status. Albany has three libraries: the University Library, the Dewey Graduate Library (for the fields of social welfare, criminal justice, information science, and public policy), and the Science Library. The library director holds the title dean of libraries and is a member of the campus deans council.

Early Information Literacy Efforts

The following sections will describe information literacy activities which were successful and unsuccessful. As experience has shown, several factors must be in place for success to occur.

What Worked, to a Degree

Before the term *information literacy* became current, *library instruction*, or *bibliographic instruction*, was the label given to the instruction that librarians provided. While the concepts of information literacy and library instruction are not synonymous, information literacy efforts have not sprung from a vacuum. In the 1980s, prior to my arrival at Albany, there was a mandatory freshman composition course that included a library component. This component involved a workbook that all students had to complete satisfactorily. Once the composition course requirement was abolished, new models of library instruction were needed. There was no other required course with which to link in order to instruct all incoming first-year students. A new, dual-pronged approach was taken: both course-related instruction and library-sponsored classes that anyone might attend were offered.

Course-related instruction is designed to meet the needs of students as they relate to a course assignment. Students' motivation is often high, because what they learn has an immediate use. However, this type of instruction depends upon faculty members seeing a need for it and being willing to relinquish one or two class periods for the instruction sessions. It was very difficult at Albany, with such a large faculty, to have an impact on many students with this type of instruction. Its implementation was hit or miss, with some faculty members requesting it regularly and others, whose students might well have benefited, not availing themselves of the service.

The library-sponsored classes began in the early 1990s, when technology was starting to have a massive impact on methods of doing research. CD-ROM databases were newly available for searching, to be followed a few years later by the nascent Internet. The classes we offered focused on these and other technologies, such as searching the on-line catalog effectively, and also on introducing key electronic resources in a variety of disciplines. Initially, the classes were highly popular with graduate, international, and returning students. These students knew that they would need to understand these information systems and were willing to take the time beforehand to learn what they needed to know. As the technologies have become ubiquitous, demand for these sessions has declined.

What Didn't Work

Although the instructional efforts just described were in place, the dean of libraries recognized that a more coherent effort to address information and computer literacy was needed. The existing range of library and computing services instruction was not "integrated into the General Education curriculum or other academic curriculum" (Butler and others, 1993). In 1992, the dean of libraries and the director of computing and network services co-chaired the Information Literacy Committee, which was made up of faculty members, computing services professionals, and librarians and was charged with developing "an integrated plan for enabling faculty and students to become skilled at identifying, evaluating, managing and using a rich and diverse array of information sources" (Butler and others, 1993). The committee's report proposed a set of standards for undergraduate students in three areas: computer literacy, information acquisition, and networking. It also outlined plans for addressing students' instructional needs. One plan outlined methods to teach seven basic skill areas, including electronic mail, file management, text management, and Internet resources. It was recognized that some students would need to learn some or all of these skills in order to be successful in electronic educational and work environments. Another plan proposed a model for grounding information literacy instruction in the major. While members of the Undergraduate Academic Council and the University Senate felt that the plan had great merit, none of the committee's recommendations were mandated by these governance bodies. Without such a mandate, it was not possible to initiate the comprehensive package of recommendations.

In 1995, the SUNY Council of Library Directors created four systemwide task forces to address issues related to libraries and to information access and skills. I was appointed to the Task Force on Information Skills of Faculty and Students, which included librarians, SUNY administrators, and representatives from key SUNY-wide organizations and from the City University of New York. The task force's charge was "to develop recommendations that when implemented will provide SUNY faculty and students with appropriate information skills." Unfortunately, the task force was too large to address its charge effectively.

In 1996, the SUNY Council of Library Directors formed a new body, the Information Literacy Initiative Committee. This group, smaller and more nimble than the 1995 task force, consisted of faculty members and librarians from several institutions in the system, including a faculty member who is now the dean of undergraduate studies at Albany. It was charged with the following tasks:

- Identify desired information literacy competencies across the curriculum

- Develop a process to implement a systemwide information literacy initiative in SUNY institutions

- Promote the adoption of the desired information literacy competencies across the curricula

- Develop an advocacy program that publicizes to SUNY faculty the principles of information literacy, especially in relation to accreditation. The intended audience also included librarians, the University Faculty Senate, academic vice presidents, the SUNY Council of Presidents, and other appropriate groups.

- Share information about successful and model programs among SUNY campuses via the Web and listservs (Glogowski and others, 1997)

The committee members developed a list of nine information literacy competencies with detailed indicators to show how a student could meet each competency. They also developed recommendations for outreach to and support for faculty, for integration of information literacy competencies into the curriculum, for developing a SUNY information literacy advocacy program, and for developing a Web site to share information about successful programs and models. The report is available at http://www.sunyconnect.suny.edu/ili/final.htm. The work of this group had an impact on individual campuses, librarians, and faculty members throughout the system. Members of the Library Instruction Committee of the SUNY Librarians Association created a Web page (http://library.lib.binghamton.edu/sunyla/curriculum. html) that lists sample assignments and teaching methods for each of the nine competencies. Some individual pieces of the recommendations were acted upon at Albany; however, the full scope of the recommendations, particularly in regard to integrating information literacy initiatives into the curriculum, was difficult to implement without a directive from a campus administrator or governance body.

Current Information Literacy Program

Often, it takes more than desire to implement an information literacy program. Sometimes, it takes the decision of a governing board to mandate change.

Board of Trustee Mandate

The current general education requirement that all Albany students, in their first or second year, take an information literacy course, did not arise directly from either the 1992–93 or the 1997 committee or task force recommendations. Rather, it came from SUNY's board of trustees. They passed a resolution (no. 98–241) in 1998 establishing a core general education program for all SUNY institutions. This general education program laid out requirements for ten knowledge and skill areas (for example, history and foreign languages) and two competencies, information management and critical thinking. The board of trustees mandated that these programs be in place by the fall 2000 semester. Each individual campus was to determine how it would meet the new requirements. While this new core general education program provoked heated discussion and debate on numerous campuses (many of which had their own previously established general education programs), librarians and others were encouraged that one of the skill areas was information management, which was defined as follows:

Students will:

- perform the basic operations of personal computer use;

- understand and use basic research techniques; and

- locate, evaluate and synthesize information from a variety of sources. [Provost's Advisory Task Force on General Education, 1999]

Because each institution was free to develop institution-specific methods to meet this requirement, it was interpreted in different ways on various campuses. Albany began to work on defining this skill area right away. When the board of trustees later clarified that the learning outcomes for the competencies might be accomplished by completing assignments spread throughout the overall general education curriculum, the model of meeting the requirement through taking a specific course had already been accepted on campus.

Information Literacy Requirement

Albany not only retained the course requirement for this skill area, but also changed its name from *information management* to *information literacy*. Members of the committee who were developing the guidelines felt that *information management* was too restrictive a term and that the skills they would like students to master were better encompassed under the term *information literacy*. The description of information literacy courses explains just what knowledge and skills students will learn in these courses: "Information Literacy: approved courses describe the processes of finding, organizing, using, producing and distributing information in a variety of media formats, including traditional print as well as computer databases; students acquire experience with resources available on the Internet; students learn to evaluate the quality of information, to work ethically and professionally, and to adjust to rapidly changing technology tools" (University at Albany, State University of New York, 2001, p. 49).

The original guidelines stipulated that courses that met this new general education requirement would have three characteristics:

- Lectures on finding, citing, evaluating, and using information in print and electronic sources from the University Libraries, World Wide Web, electronic databases, and other sources. Courses should address questions concerning the ethical use of information, responsible computing, copyright, and other related issues that promote critical reflection;

- Assignments and course work that make extensive use of the University Libraries, World Wide Web, and other information sources. Assignments should include finding, evaluating, and citing information sources;

- One or more assignments on the research process including developing an annotated bibliography that requires the student to find, evaluate, use, and cite information resources. [University at Albany, 2000]

During the 2001–2002 academic year, the guidelines were changed. In the first guideline, "lectures" became "classroom activities." In the second guideline, tutorials were added to assignments and coursework. The third guideline was rewritten: "At least one research project that requires students to find, evaluate, cite, and use information presented in diverse formats from multiple sources and to integrate this information within a single textual, visual, or digital document." These new guidelines provide more flexibility for instructors and allow them to develop research projects that meet the information literacy goals but also fit their discipline better than an annotated bibliography might.

Librarians' Involvement

Librarians' earlier efforts in library instruction and information literacy had not gone unnoticed on campus. The dean of libraries is an extremely effective advocate for librarians and their teaching responsibilities, stressing their unique knowledge base. It was strategic, too, that the faculty member from Albany who had served on the 1996–1997 SUNY Council of Library Directors Information Literacy Initiative Committee was now the dean of undergraduate studies. It was the responsibility of her office to implement the new general education requirements.

The dean of libraries, the assistant director of user services, and the coordinator of user education programs (me) were all invited to meet with the dean of undergraduate studies and the associate dean for general education. These two campus administrators were strong advocates for librarians being closely involved with the new information literacy requirement. They were interested in librarians offering small sections of a course that would meet the new requirement. During the meeting, other models of instruction were also discussed, including librarians partnering with faculty members to integrate information literacy into existing courses and librarians offering one-credit enhancements for targeted courses in order to meet the requirement for interested students.

The administration provided critical support to the libraries by funding two FTE librarian instructors and an extremely well-equipped computer classroom with twenty-three student computers (despite the injunction that the new general education program was to be implemented with no new resources).

The Information Literacy Subcommittee

The Information Literacy Subcommittee, which is advisory to the General Education Committee, was formed to provide oversight for the information literacy requirement. The subcommittee is made up of the associate dean for general education, faculty members, and librarians. It reviews the criteria for courses that meet the information literacy requirement and also reviews course proposals. The chair of the subcommittee, a faculty member who himself teaches an information literacy course, has also publicized the general education information literacy component, with invitations to faculty members to submit course proposals. A continuing concern is the availability of sufficient seats in information literacy courses for approximately two thousand students each year.

Information Literacy Courses

There are a number of courses that fulfill the information literacy general education requirement. They vary in credit hours and in size, from small hands-on classes to an enormous lecture center class of almost five hundred students. Some are offered by departments and are closely tied to a discipline, while others are generic. Some do a better job of meeting the information literacy course requirements than others (a review of courses in several years' time will, it is hoped, correct the imbalances in student learning). Students are free to select the course that they will take to meet the requirement.

   UNL 205, Information Literacy   This one-credit, quarter-long course is taught by librarians. This is currently the only information literacy course that earns only one credit or lasts less than a full semester. It is designed to be small (no more than twenty-three students, frequently fewer), to be hands-on, and to actively engage students. It is generic in the skills it teaches, but students are encouraged to pick an annotated bibliography topic based on work they are doing in another course. Approximately forty sections of the course are taught each year. UNL 206, Information Literacy and the Sciences, debuted in 2002. It is a one-credit course which lasts a quarter.

   AAS 240/LCS 240/WSS 240, Classism, Racism, and Sexism   One professor's section of this course, which is cross-listed in the Africana Studies, Latin American and Caribbean Studies, and Women's Studies departments, meets the information literacy requirement through class activities, use of tutorials, and an assignment.

CSI 198T, Microcomputer Consulting Services in the University Library   Students, who can take this course for either two or three credits, receive extensive hands-on training in order to assist fellow students in using computing stations in the reference area of the University Library. As part of this training, they receive extensive information literacy instruction and complete assignments as stipulated in the requirements.

EAS 205, East Asian Research and Bibliographic Methods   This new course was designed specifically to meet the new information literacy requirement for students majoring in East Asian Studies. Nonmajors with one year of Chinese, Japanese, or Korean are also eligible for the course, which teaches students the specialized knowledge required to do research in their field. Students spend a good deal of time in the library practicing the use of research tools. The final project is an annotated bibliography that includes different types of resources.

ECPY 204, Principles of Career and Life Planning   This is a multiple-section course taught by graduate students. However, because the instructors are closely overseen by a faculty member in the School of Education's Department of Counseling Psychology, the course sections are carefully standardized. Information literacy activities include a lecture on plagiarism by a member of the Writing Center, a class on the APA style of citation and the ethical use of information, a trip to the Career Development Center for an introduction to career resources in print and electronic formats, and a class by a librarian on information sources available through the libraries. Students also complete at least one tutorial offered by the University Library and write a report on an academic or occupational area of interest, using a variety of information sources.

GOG 160M/EAC 160M, China in the Post-Utopian Age   This course, offered through both the Geography and Planning and the East Asian Studies departments, is a fairly large lecture class. Students in this course are taught twice by a librarian. They complete two tutorials, as well as mapping and film exercises and two research projects that require the use of a variety of research sources. The information literacy component of this course was developed through close collaboration between the geography bibliographer (subject specialist) and the course professor.

ISP 100, Internet and Information Access   The title and content of this course offered by the School of Information Science and Policy ensure that students will flock to register. The course also serves as the introduction to the growing information science undergraduate major. The professor who teaches the course refers to it as "driver's ed for the Internet." It is taught in a lecture hall and has a maximum enrollment of just under five hundred students. Students learn about both Internet- and non-Internet-based methods of doing research, and the final project is an annotated bibliography on a topic of the student's choice. The professor of this course works closely with librarians, because the number of his students has an enormous impact on the number of questions fielded by reference librarians.

ISP 301, The Information Environment   This lecture hall course is required for information science majors. It introduces them to the field "through the discussion, analysis, evaluation, and production of information in various forms (from print to digital)." In spring 2002, this course made use of the recently expanded scope of the final project beyond an annotated bibliography. Students were assigned to write an essay, formatted in HTML, on a research topic related to the information environment, using eight different types of information sources. Students in this course complete the tutorials "Researching 101" and "Evaluating Internet Sites 101."

LIN 100M, Understanding Language   In this introductory course, students learn how to find, cite, and evaluate a variety of information sources related to appropriate topics. They also learn about the social and ethical issues surrounding information. The course includes an annotated bibliography as the final project.

UNI 100, The Freshman Year Experience   This three-credit, multiple-section course is designed to help freshmen become more effective as students. Unlike in Principles of Career and Life Planning (ECPY 204), the sections are not currently standardized in regard to their information literacy instruction. This is unfortunate, because this course might be an excellent venue for such instruction. Students in most sections are required to work through one or more of the tutorials offered by the library, but research assignments beyond the tutorials vary.

UNI 151–158, Project Renaissance   Project Renaissance is a freshman-year experience program enrolling approximately four hundred students annually. Students earn six credits for each of two semesters of Project Renaissance coursework. They enroll in pre-professional sections (for example, pre-law or pre-business) and take a linked course in the appropriate discipline. Information literacy instruction is folded into the program over the full course of the year and is targeted to each section's field of interest.

WSS 109N, Women, Biology and Health   Information literacy activities and assignments are integrated throughout this women's studies course, culminating in a group assignment in which students work in mock policymaking committees on a health topic.

Resources Available to Assist Faculty Members

The Information Literacy Subcommittee would like to encourage instructors of appropriate discipline-based courses to consider revising their courses to meet the information literacy requirements. Information literacy courses that relate directly to a student's major are ideal. Student motivation is high in these settings, because students immediately understand the worth of what they are learning. The Association of College and Research Libraries (2000) notes, "Achieving competency in information literacy requires an understanding that this cluster of abilities is not extraneous to the curriculum but is woven into the curriculum's content, structure, and sequence." Faculty members, however, are often wary of redesigning their courses around a content area in which they might not feel themselves to be expert. The Center for Excellence in Teaching and Learning (CETL) and the University Libraries both provide a number of resources for faculty who are interested in qualifying or have already qualified their class to fulfill the information literacy requirement.

The Center for Excellence in Teaching and Learning

The CETL supports the information literacy requirement by providing a wide range of assistance to faculty members, including workshops, digital classrooms, and teaching and technology assistance.

Workshops   The CETL offers short workshops on a wide variety of topics that interest teaching faculty. One that is offered frequently is on plagiarism, a prime concern of all faculty members and a topic that is often addressed formally in information literacy courses. The CETL also routinely offers a session on what is needed for a class to fulfill the information literacy requirement. This session is attended by the chair of the Information Literacy Subcommittee, the coordinator of user education programs (me), and often other members of the subcommittee. These resource people are able to explain the various requirements and answer specific questions from interested faculty. Another workshop, Best Practices in Information Literacy, was offered during fall 2002. This workshop involved three pairs of faculty members and librarians describing their cooperative work on a course. This session was designed to provide ideas to others who already teach or plan to teach an information literacy course. A third fall 2002 workshop, designed for a broader audience, focused on assignments that make heavy use of the University Libraries, which include some of those given in information literacy courses. Librarians discussed ways that they can assist faculty members when they develop research assignments so that students do not encounter undue frustrations.

Classrooms   The CETL makes available two large (forty-seat) digital classrooms. Because information literacy courses often require hands-on computer work, these classrooms are important to meeting the needs of these courses.

Teaching and Technology Assistance   CETL staff members are available to consult with faculty members and teaching assistants on teaching and classroom issues. They also help with WebCT implementation and the design of course Web pages.

University Libraries

Librarians feel a close connection to information literacy efforts throughout the campus. Information literacy instruction is a key component of our profession, be it in our own classrooms, in guest lectures in a course in a discipline, at the reference desk, or in the research that we do. Librarians provide a number of resources to interested faculty members and teaching assistants that can ease the work when crafting a course to meet the information literacy guidelines.

Information Literacy Tutorials

One issue faced by research institutions when implementing information literacy programs is scalability. Scalability can be a challenge in a number of arenas, but one of them usually involves the number of librarians able to participate and the amount of time they can devote to the program. Albany librarians have developed a number of tutorials that have been critical to the expansion of the information literacy program on campus. These tutorials cover some of the key components that students need to know, freeing a librarian or the course instructor from having to teach this material directly. Each tutorial has a feedback form at the end, which sends a message to the library confirming that the student has completed it. A graduate student collects this information and sends it to each instructor. A number of instructors assign one or more of the tutorials for course points. The tutorials, available at http://library.albany.edu/usered/tut.html, are as follows:

Researching 101   This tutorial introduces students to the concept of information formats and the need to determine which format is appropriate for a particular need or type of information. Students also learn how to use the on-line catalogue and electronic databases, including how to develop effective search strategies, and they learn the differences between the catalogue and the article databases.

Evaluating Internet Sites 101   This tutorial teaches students the importance of evaluating materials found on the Web and provides key criteria that students should ascertain before deciding on the value of a Web site. Students are also encouraged to apply what they learn to other information formats. This tutorial has been assigned by faculty members around the country, since it is not institution-specific.

Virtual Tour   This tour is specific to the University Library; it highlights a number of services and resources with which many students are unfamiliar.

Plagiarism 101   A new addition to our collection of tutorials, this one became available in fall 2002, after being tested by students in a course during the summer. This tutorial, which introduces students to the various forms of plagiarism, the penalties involved, and strategies to avoid plagiarizing, has already become popular, given the extreme importance of the topic in the Web environment.

Each tutorial takes twenty to forty minutes to complete. All contain screen shots, photographs, or other graphics to illustrate the intellectual content. They also require students to answer questions in order to proceed through the material, to encourage students to engage with the content.

Other Web-Based and Print-Based Guides

Librarians have long offered a number of bibliographies, guides, and how-to sheets on a variety of research topics. While these were once only offered in print format, most have now been mounted electronically as well. The most popular amongst these guides are those detailing the MLA and APA citation styles, how to write annotated bibliography entries, and how to distinguish between scholarly and popular periodicals. Librarians frequently create new guides based on the needs of students in information literacy courses. During the summer of 2002, interactive Web pages on how to read a citation and on the differences between popular and scholarly periodicals were developed. In addition, a set of guide sheets were written to aid students in their search for the items mostly commonly required for annotated bibliographies (such as a scholarly Web site, a news or general interest Web site, a reference source, a scholarly print journal article, an article or column from both print and on-line newspapers, and so on). While these guides, both printed and on the Web, are aimed particularly at students in Internet and Information Access (ISP 100), the large lecture class, they are available to any faculty member or student who might find them useful.

Pairing with a Librarian

Both instruction librarians and bibliographers are available to work closely with faculty members as they design or teach an information literacy course. Instruction librarians frequently work with a faculty member on the initial development of coursework or assignments that are needed to meet the information literacy requirement. Bibliographers may also become involved at this stage; in addition, they often teach one or two class sessions. These sessions may consist of introducing key resources such as the on-line catalogue or discipline-specific databases, or teaching students how to evaluate the information that they find.

Reference Assistance

Information literacy courses have a heavy impact on librarians who provide reference assistance in the three libraries. Course assignments require students to use a variety of resources, and while some of these may be available remotely, students need to use the libraries at least part of the time. Librarians are happy to assist students, but both librarians and students may become frustrated when long lines form at the reference desk just before an information literacy assignment is due. The more closely faculty members and librarians interact, the smoother reference assistance can be. Cooperation has led to revised assignments, changed due dates, and other measures that have strengthened the librarians' ability to provide direct help to students. For example, one day, a large number of students from one course all arrived at the reference desk with questions about how to find a print scholarly article. To cope with the heavy demand, two librarians began offering drop-in sessions, heavily advertised at the reference desk, in class, and on the course Web page, to teach a number of students at once about the most effective ways to complete this assignment.

Resource Web Page

I have developed a Web page (http://library.albany.edu/usered/faculty/infolit.html) that serves as a guide to information literacy resources, both those on campus and those developed by other institutions and professional associations. This page provides information on and links to the information literacy requirements, ways in which librarians can assist faculty members, tutorials from both Albany and the University of Texas that can be assigned to students, the Association of College and Research Libraries' *Information Literacy Competency Standards for Higher Education* document, and the "Curriculum Relevant to the SUNY Council of Library Directors Information Literacy Initiative" Web page.

Student Reactions

There has been no formal survey of students about the information literacy requirement. Feedback has come through course evaluation forms, written responses to the tutorials, and in comments made to faculty members teaching information literacy courses.

In the first two years of teaching Information Literacy (UNL 205), librarians found that the students who most appreciated the coursework were actually juniors or seniors. While students at this level were not required to take an information literacy course (in the first three years of the requirement, they were exempt entirely, because the requirement was introduced with the class of 2004), they had sufficient experience with writing research papers to grasp how much they did not know. They understood how much time they would have saved and how they might have selected better resources if they had had an information literacy course earlier in their academic career. Many of these students explicitly stated, in front of other students or on evaluation forms, that this should have been required of them when they started at the university. Ironically, it is the freshmen in our courses who often do not see the immediate need for what they are learning, particularly if they are not enrolled in a course that requires a research paper or project. While the UNL 205 assignment attempts to maximize relevance of the final annotated bibliography by encouraging students to tie it into an assignment in another course, this is not possible if there is no such assignment. A few students have commented that they already knew everything taught in the course. They may have been familiar with the topics, but assessment has shown that they did increase their skills and critical abilities.

When students in the Internet and Information Access class (ISP 100) are asked, on the last day of class, what they have learned in the course, a number of them are surprised at how much they have learned. When they registered for the course, they were certain of their Internet skills (after all, they use it all the time), but during the course, they found that there was much that was new to them.

Professors of other information literacy courses agree that most students react favorably to this general education requirement. Students in Understanding Language (LIN 100M) enjoy the content of the course and find the issues that they study—language and gender, language and advertising, and dialects—to be extremely engaging. They appreciate the opportunity to find additional resources on these subjects, either in cases where they are particularly interested in a topic and want to learn more or when they are exploring various topics to select one for further study. The professor believes that this course provides a natural home for the information literacy component and has found some students to be "inspired" by learning about the information resources available to them.

The professor teaching The Information Environment (ISP 301) echoes this thought: "Students seem to gain a real sense of empowerment when they learn how to find information that was previously unavailable to them" (Thomas Mackey, personal communication, Aug. 28, 2002). He feels that most students respond favorably to the information literacy requirement, but some would prefer to focus on technology skills development.

Students in discipline-based courses often understand more immediately the need to become information literate when it has a direct impact on their work in the course. While students in the generic information literacy course (UNL 205) frequently come to realize that they are learning valuable skills, this connection often comes when they use these skills in another course.

The other feedback we have from students has been collected through pages on the Web-based tutorials that specifically solicit students' comments. While these comments apply to the tutorials rather than to the broader information literacy requirement, they provide one piece of evidence about student reactions. The vast majority of the comments have been positive, particularly on the Evaluating Internet Sites 101 and Virtual Tour tutorials. Students appreciate learning how to judge the Web pages that they use so heavily both when doing research and in non-academic searches for information. They are also excited to learn about less traditional resources available through the libraries, such as DVDs, videos, music CDs, scanners, and classes on developing Web pages. Early feedback about the Plagiarism 101 tutorial, when it was being reviewed in draft form, was very positive. A number of students mentioned that they had not been aware of the variety of activities that can be labeled plagiarism, even though they were in their junior or senior year. Several students strongly recommended that lower-level undergraduate students be required to complete the tutorial.

Assessing Information Literacy Instruction

A three-year review cycle of the general education program began in fall 2002. Information literacy courses will be reviewed during the third year. It is expected that at that time, courses that have never fully instituted the course guidelines will be flagged, so that they can be re-reviewed or redesigned to meet the requirements. This review will also provide data on the effectiveness of the instruction. In the interim, assessment is left to the discretion of the instructors.

UNL 205 uses both formal and informal assessment methods. Students are given a pretest on the first day of class. The questions are closely aligned with the material taught during the course, and the results do provide evidence that some students are familiar with some of the topics that are covered in the course. An identical posttest is given on the last day of the course. Correct answers consistently increase from pretest to posttest. UNL 205 instructors have gained valuable insights about course topics and the effectiveness of our instruction based on the pretest and posttest results. We have varied the amount of time spent on certain areas, spending less time on topics students uniformly seem to know at the start of the course.

We use a variety of informal assessment methods throughout the course. Many UNL 205 instructors ask students to do freewriting or engage in activities where student learning is immediately obvious (for instance, inserting Boolean operators into search strings to obtain optimum results). At the course midpoint, I ask students to work in small groups to develop concept maps based on the topics that have been covered in the course. Although these concept maps are not graded, they allow me to quickly see whether students are making the appropriate connections among course topics. The hands-on, active learning focus of the course makes incorporating such informal assessment activities easy to accomplish.

The professor who teaches Internet and Information Access (ISP 100) has, through informal assessment, found that a significant number of students are not cognizant of what a browser is or what the difference is between the World Wide Web and the Internet. These are concepts that one might expect all students to know. This finding has affected the way that the early sessions of the course are taught.

Thomas Mackey, who teaches The Information Environment (ISP 301), comments on an assessment tool he uses:

> I conduct a fairly extensive technology/information literacy survey at the beginning and end of the course. I am very interested in finding out where students are when they enter the course so that I can have a sense of my audience even before I start to lecture or develop assignments. Although the syllabus is in place before the class starts, I can tailor my teaching approach to each class based on the survey. Since I share the results of the survey with the class, students have also told me that the survey helps them to realize that they are not the only ones who need to learn these skills. So many students make the assumption that they are the only ones who do not know how to use technology or conduct research that I think the survey helps to reinforce the fact that this is a learning community with specific learning goals.
>
> The exit survey helps me to assess student learning based on very specific categories (HTML knowledge, UNIX experience, research skills). Students have also commented in the open-ended questions at the end of the survey that they did not realize how much they had learned in the class until they took the time to respond

to each question and that the vast number of skills addressed in the survey helped them to see their accomplishments. In this case, the assessment was as much a valuable tool for the students as it was for me. [Thomas Mackey, personal communication, Aug. 28, 2002]

Next Steps

The information literacy program at the University at Albany has come a long way in just a few years. The undergraduate information literacy requirement is firmly established, and the guidelines for these information literacy courses are appropriate. More courses are being developed or revised to meet these guidelines, to offer students a choice in how they meet this general education requirement. Albany's information literacy program was honored with selection, along with just nine other institutions, for the Best Practices in Information Literacy Invitational Conference sponsored by the Association of College and Research Libraries in 2002. However, there are a number of areas in which Albany could improve.

- *More gateway courses in the disciplines.* Although courses such as Understanding Language (LIN 100M), East Asian Research and Bibliographic Methods (EAS 205), and China in the Post-Utopian Age (GOG/EAC 160M) exist to meet the information literacy requirement for students planning to major in their respective disciplines, many departments do not offer an information literacy course at the freshman or sophomore level. The Information Literacy Subcommittee, the CETL, and the University Libraries are making efforts to encourage more faculty members to offer such courses. The one-credit lab option, mentioned above but not yet instituted, might provide a model for enabling more courses to meet the information literacy requirements. This model, however, depends on having bibliographers to teach the lab sections. In a climate where new personnel are not available, this might be difficult to institute.

• *Information literacy instruction in upper-division courses.* The board of trustees' resolution did not address information literacy needs beyond the general education program. Students in upper-division undergraduate courses often have information literacy needs that are more specific than those taught in lower-division undergraduate courses. The Information Environment (ISP 301) is an example of an upper-division course that goes beyond what is taught in Internet and Information Access (ISP 100) to meet the needs of majors who are learning about information science as an academic discipline and as a profession. Not all upper-division courses that teach additional information literacy skills would need to meet the general education requirement, as ISP 301 happens to do.

• *Information literacy instruction for graduate students.* Graduate students often have information literacy needs that are not being addressed. This varies by department and depending on the backgrounds of individual graduate students. The Dewey Graduate Library offers short sessions to teach new graduate students about key information resources in their fields. Some departments also address this need through particular courses. However, more opportunities for graduate students to increase their information literacy skills would be helpful.

Two areas have not yet been discussed but that would be appropriate areas for improvement are the following:

• *Postgraduation assessment of information literacy skills.* It would be useful to include information literacy questions on the surveys that are sent to Albany students after they graduate (starting after 2004). These questions might ask about the information literacy knowledge and skills that students gained while at the university and the applicability of those skills to their jobs or to graduate study. This would provide extremely important information for future reviews of the information literacy requirements.

- *Testing out of the information literacy requirement.* Some institutions with an information literacy course requirement allow students to fulfill the requirement by passing a test. There is some concern at Albany that students who take advantage of such an option would miss critical instruction that might not be adequately reflected in the test. If this option were considered, the test would have to be carefully designed to mitigate this concern.

Lessons for Other Institutions

Some aspects of Albany's situation are unique. Most institutions will not find their board of trustees mandating a new general education program that includes an information literacy component. On many campuses, the decision on an information literacy requirement will come through a more usual faculty governance process or from an effort on the part of an academic vice president or possibly a library director. Other campuses may also decide that formal information literacy courses are not the direction to take. They may opt for infusing information literacy instruction throughout the curriculum or into particular courses. Despite these campus variations, some lessons that we have learned might be of use at other institutions.

- *Make information literacy a campus concern.* When information literacy was a concern primarily of librarians, the base was not sufficiently broad to have an effect on campus culture. Meritorious efforts were undertaken, but they did not succeed in integrating information literacy into the general education curriculum. With the new mandated general education program, information literacy became an issue of importance to campus administrators and faculty members, as well as librarians. It was understood that the campus as a whole was responsible for ensuring that students become information literate.
- *Involve all constituencies during implementation of the program.* Administrators, faculty members, librarians, and others (such as

teaching center staff) all come to the issue of information literacy with different viewpoints, needs, and talents. Only by listening to all constituencies will an effective program emerge.

• *Have a small committee provide oversight.* The Information Literacy Subcommittee, made up of an administrator, faculty members, and librarians, has been able to act quickly because of its relatively small size (six to eight people). The expertise of the members has been critical in decisions about revising course requirement guidelines.

• *Do not leave out the librarians.* Information literacy is a key area within librarianship, and there will be librarians at most institutions with particular expertise in this area. There has been a great deal of research done in information literacy, and many publications, conferences, and committees exist to address the issues. Librarians will bring knowledge of these resources to the table. They will also be able to bolster information literacy initiatives by providing assistance both directly in the classroom and through support materials.

• *Support instructors who are teaching information literacy.* Provide workshops and classroom space according to particular needs of information literacy instructors. If possible, provide release time to help them effectively incorporate information literacy into their courses. Teaching assistants can help a great deal if courses have hands-on components or increased enrollments based on new requirements.

• *Support librarians who are supporting other faculty members.* The amount of time needed to support full-fledged information literacy programs can be phenomenal. It is unrealistic to expect librarians to add these responsibilities to an already full job description. New librarians may need to be hired or existing responsibilities may need to be reassigned or dropped entirely in order for librarians to be able to focus on campuswide information literacy initiatives.

• *Evaluate information literacy courses and instruction and assess student learning.* Revisit courses that focus on or include information literacy instruction. Check to see if they are still doing what they said they would do. Assess student learning to make sure that the instruction they are getting is effective. Student needs and knowledge change, especially in this fast-moving area.

Conclusion

It has taken the time and the efforts of a wide range of players, but after years of effort, information literacy has come into its own at the University at Albany. Many of the hurdles we have faced are common to all research institutions, involving faculty and administrative buy-in, size of the target population, integration into the academic program (in our case, the general education program), and addressing the importance of communication. There have been some growing pains, but the information literacy general education requirement is now a fact of life on campus, with quality courses in place to meet students' needs. These course offerings will continue to expand, and delivery methods for the instruction may change over time. Students graduating in 2004 and later will leave the institution with knowledge and a skill set for lifelong learning that was only taught in a more haphazard manner before the institution of this requirement. It will be interesting to see where we are in five or ten years, but it is certain that the program will be flexible enough to keep up with evolving information resources.

References

Association of College and Research Libraries. *Information Literacy Competency Standards for Higher Education*. Chicago: Association of College and Research Libraries, 2000. Also available at—http://www.ala.org/Content/NavigationMenu/ACRL/Standards_and_Guidelines/Information_Literacy_Competency_Standards_for_Higher_Education.htm. Accessed Aug. 26, 2002.

Butler, Meredith, and others. *Information Literacy Committee Report and Recommendations for Action*. Albany, N.Y.: University at Albany, 1993.

Glogowski, Maryruth, and others. "SUNY Council of Library Directors Information Literacy Initiative Final Report." 1997. http://www.sunyconnect.suny.edu/ili/final.htm. Accessed Aug. 8, 2002.

Orme, Bill. "First Year Connections: Establishing Comprehensive Links to the University, Services, and Community." 1999. http://www-lib.iupui. edu/itt/scremark.html. Accessed Sept. 24, 2002.

Provost's Advisory Task Force on General Education. "Implementation Guidelines for State University of New York Baccalaureate Candidate General Education Requirement." 1999. http://www.sunysb.edu/provost/Reports/ GenEdReq/gened-curr.doc. Accessed Aug. 30, 2002.

University at Albany, State University of New York. *Communication and Reasoning Competencies: Information Literacy.* " Unpublished document. Albany, N.Y.: University of Albany, 2000.

University at Albany, State University of New York. "The New General Education Program: Communication and Reasoning Competencies Categories: Information Literacy." In *Undergraduate Bulletin* 2001-2002 (p. 49). Albany, N.Y.: University at Albany, 2001.

6

Developing a Tool to Assess Community College Students

Bonnie Gratch-Lindauer, Amelie Brown

The Bay Area California Community Colleges Information Competency Assessment Project evolved out of a number of activities under way at one of the San Francisco Bay Area community colleges, Diablo Valley College (DVC), and important statewide initiatives related to making information competency a graduation requirement for the Associate of Arts and Associate of Science degrees at all 108 California community colleges.

At several points in this three-year project, librarians collaborated across higher education segments and with their respective faculties to define standards and performance outcomes suitable for California community college students, as well as react to drafts of the information competency proficiency exam. Diablo Valley College was among a small number of California community colleges awarded three Student Success grants from the California Community Colleges' State Chancellor's Office in fall 1999 to integrate information competency into the college's instructional offerings and to promote it to other educational institutions. These three grants allowed DVC to expand and develop its information competency instructional offerings to English as a Second Language (ESL) and basic skills students; to develop a new one-credit course for students working at the college level; and to increase collaboration between educational institutions at various levels with regard to information competency program planning. It was this last initiative that hosted three colloquia that first brought members of what would become the information competency test development project team together for stimulating presentations and discussions on issues related to information competency.

Paralleling these grant-funded activities during the academic year 1999–2000, the DVC general education graduation requirements for Associate of Arts degrees were scheduled for review. DVC librarians proactively became engaged in review committees to advocate a new graduation requirement for information competency. DVC faculty and the Faculty Senate approved this additional graduation requirement in the spring of 2000, and the new requirement became effective in fall 2003.

At nearby Santa Rosa Junior College, the library faculty were also working with their academic senate and its curriculum committee throughout the 2000–2001 academic year to institute an information competency requirement in the college's general education curriculum. This was approved and became effective in fall 2002. Similar efforts were under way at other Bay Area community colleges, particularly at the City College of San Francisco and Cabrillo College, which has a credit course corequisite with English 1A.

At the state level, librarians and other faculty and administrators in the California Community Colleges have addressed the need for students to possess information competency skills for nearly ten years. In 1996, the State Chancellor's Office of the California Community Colleges identified information competency as a systemwide priority. Between 1996 and 1999, several reports and resolutions discussed implementation. In April 2001, the Curriculum Committee of the Statewide Academic Senate passed a resolution approving information competency as a "locally designed graduation requirement." A State Chancellor's Office task force prepared language, which was near approval by the state board of governors, to revise Title 5 of the *California Code of Regulations*. However, the California Department of Finance determined that the fiscal impact might be difficult to fund, so the initiative has been put on hold.[1]

All of these activities provided a ripe environment in which librarians could share information and strategies about their initiatives and also address a common need: a proficiency exam that students could pass in order to satisfy the anticipated graduation requirement. Therefore, several meetings of interested Bay Area community college and California State University (CSU) librarians were held, in order to share information and discuss approaches for building on the information competency momentum that was building locally, regionally, statewide, and nationally. Discussions centered on how to define information competency skills as measurable outcomes; strategies for encouraging acceptance among other faculty and administrators; and effective teaching strategies and materials. A librarian from City College of San Francisco encouraged the formation of a working group to explore assessment of information competency. As this issue was explored, the need and mutual interests pointed to the desire to develop a challenge-out test for the information competency requirement, because several librarians were planning for implementation of a campus information competency requirement. (Earning course credit through a challenge exam is equivalent to passing a cumulative, end-of-the-term examination or a series of comparable exams which are course requirements.) Librarians from five institutions—City College of San Francisco, Diablo Valley College, Cabrillo College, Santa Rosa Junior College, and CSU Monterey Bay—formed the project team, with librarians from several other community colleges and neighboring California State University campuses serving as contributors. This group did not define its charge to reflect the needs or situations of all California community colleges; instead, to maintain a manageable project, the scope was limited to developing and field-testing an instrument for use as a challenge-out exam for interested Bay Area community colleges, with the understanding that the final exam would be of interest to and adaptable by others.

Identifying the Exam's Purpose, Standards, and Criteria

Once the project team members[2] had agreed on the purpose of the exam (a mechanism for students to use to satisfy the anticipated graduation requirement in information competency) and that the exam would be criterion-referenced (it measures how well individual students do relative to pre-determined performance levels, knowledge, or skills), the next step was to specify the standards and criteria for which exam items would be developed. Fortunately, two major Association of College and Research Libraries (ACRL) documents had recently been published: *Information Literacy Competency Standards for Higher Education* (Association of College and Research Libraries, 2000), which has also been endorsed by the American Association for Higher Education, and "Objectives for Information Literacy Instruction: A Model Statement for Academic Librarians" (Association of College and Research Libraries, 2001). This important step involved the project team spending several months discussing how to adapt the indicators and outcomes from these two ACRL documents. Decisions were based on which outcomes were appropriate for community college students. The team also closely reviewed two local adaptations of the ACRL documents, which had been created with input from discipline-based faculty at Diablo Valley College and Santa Rosa Junior College. This process resulted in several drafts and revisions. The document "Bay Area Community College Information Competency Standards, Performance Indicators and Outcomes," reflects the final consensus.[3] Exhibit 6.1 illustrates the specific performance outcomes and indicators for one of the five standards.

The consensus document reflects both what the project team felt was important for community college students' information competency and what their instructional programs currently address. While the national information competency standards document has five broad areas of performance outcomes, the project

Exhibit 6.1. Standard Two of the "Bay Area Regional Community College Information Competency Standards, Performance Indicators and Outcomes"

Standard Two: The information literate student accesses needed information effectively and efficiently.

Performance Indicators (PI):
P.I. 2.1. The information literate student selects the most appropriate investigative methods and/or information retrieval systems for accessing the needed information.

Outcomes Include:
2.1.1. Identifies the types of information contained in a particular system (e.g., all branch libraries are included in the catalogue) and the types of sources indexed in a particular database/index (e.g., full-text vs. abstract; scholarly vs. popular).
2.1.2. Selects appropriate information retrieval system(s) for research question/topic based on investigating the scope, content, organization and help features of such search tools as OPAC (Online Public Access Catalog), reference sources, periodical databases, Web, etc.
2.1.3. Identifies other investigative methods to obtain needed information not likely to be available via information retrieval systems (e.g., need to survey or interview experts, participant-observation findings, etc.).

P.I. 2.2. The information literate student constructs and implements effectively designed search strategies.

Outcomes Include:
2.2.1. Develops a research plan appropriate to the information retrieval system(s) and/or investigative method.
2.2.2. Identifies keywords, phrases, synonyms and related terms for the information needed.
2.2.3. Selects controlled vocabulary specific to the search tool and identifies where controlled vocabulary is used in an item record, and

Exhibit 6.1. Standard Two of the "Bay Area Regional Community College Information Competency Standards, Performance Indicators and Outcomes," *continued*

then successfully searches for additional information using that vocabulary.

2.2.4. Constructs and implements the search strategy using appropriate search features and commands for the information retrieval system selected (e.g., Boolean logic, truncation, field-searching, etc.).

2.2.5. Uses help screens and other user aids (e.g., reference librarians) to improve search results.

P.I. 2.3. The information literate student retrieves information online or in person using a variety of methods.

Outcomes Include:

2.3.1. Uses various search systems to retrieve information in a variety of formats such as online library catalogs, reference sources, periodical databases, Web search tools.

2.3.2. Distinguishes among citations to identify various types of materials (e.g., books, periodical articles, essays in anthologies).

2.3.3. Uses various classification schemes and other systems (e.g., call number system or indexes) to locate information resources within the library.

2.3.4. Uses specialized online or in-person services available at the institution to retrieve information needed (e.g., reference service, interlibrary loan).

P.I. 2.4. The information literate student refines the search strategy if necessary.

Outcomes Include:

2.4.1. Assesses the quantity, quality, and relevance of the search results to determine whether alternative information retrieval systems or investigative methods should be used.

2.4.2. Identifies gaps in information needed from the search results.

2.4.3. Revises the search strategy if necessary to obtain more information.

P.I. 2.5. The information literate student extracts, records, and manages the information and its sources.

Outcomes Include:
2.5.1. Records all pertinent citation information for future reference.
2.5.2. Demonstrates an understanding of how to organize information gathered (e.g., cards, file folders, etc.).
2.5.3. Differentiates between the types of sources cited and understands the elements and correct syntax of a citation for a range of sources.

Source: Based on Association of College and Research Libraries, 2000, 2001.

team realized the practical limitations of what could reasonably be assessed in an exam setting. Therefore, some performance indicators and outcomes are included in the consensus document that are not assessed on the proficiency exam—such as some for Standard Four. They are included because the project team wants their respective faculty, administrators, and curriculum specialists to be aware of all five of the national standards, since teaching students to become information literate is a role that is shared between departmental teaching faculty and librarians. To clarify this point, it is useful to take a closer look at Standard Four of the *Information Literacy Competency Standards for Higher Education* (Association of College and Research Libraries, 2000).

Standard Four of the ACRL standards states, "The information literate student, individually or as a member of a group, uses information effectively to accomplish a specific purpose." The project team felt that this standard could not be well addressed by the project's goals. Most of the performance outcomes under this standard would require some type of fairly lengthy writing and/or speaking assignment to assess. A few examples of these performance outcomes are provided to illustrate the complexity of trying to devise information competency exam items to assess them.

4.1.1. Organizes the content in a manner that supports the purposes and format of the product or performance (e.g., outlines, drafts, storyboards).

4.1.2. Articulates knowledge and skills transferred from prior experiences to plan and create the product or performance.

4.3.4. Communicates clearly and with a style that supports the purposes of the intended audience.

These types of outcomes could be better assessed in a course setting across a semester or a year through assignment-based products such as essays, research papers or research projects, or oral presentations. It might be possible, however, for an institution to combine this project's proficiency exam with some type of instrument that departmental teaching faculty have developed for assessing the types of outcomes specified in Standard Four. Other performance outcomes that were retained in the consensus document but could not be included in the proficiency exam include the following:

2.5.2. Demonstrates an understanding of how to organize information gathered (e.g. cards, file folders, etc.).

3.2.2. Analyzes the logic of arguments in the information gathered.

5.2.3. Preserves the integrity of information resources, equipment, systems, and facilities.

Design and Development of the Exam

The exam development phase involved several steps. As a first step, the project team gathered samples of library research and information literacy tests, quizzes, and performance-based assignments used at higher education institutions around the country. After this review they decided that the proficiency exam would have two parts: a cognitive part to measure what students know (Part A) and a performance-based part to measure what students can do (Part B).

The project team knew from the beginning that the expertise and services of a testing consultant would be needed to ensure that the final instrument would be well designed and scientifically valid and reliable. A subgroup of the team wrote a proposal and was awarded a research grant award for $2,000 from the California Academic and Research Libraries (CARL), a chapter of the national Association for College and Research Libraries (ACRL). This amount was supplemented later in the project by small amounts from an ACRL/IMLS (Institute for Museum and Library Services) grant and by a California Community Colleges State Chancellor's Office grant.

The second step, the actual design of exam items, was time-consuming and involved several drafts and discussions. To make the task more manageable, the team divided into two groups: one subgroup for Part A and one for Part B. For the next several months, each subgroup worked to develop the exam items, which were based directly on the consensus document of performance outcomes. Since the project team members were geographically scattered around the San Francisco Bay Area, most of the collaborative work was accomplished through e-mail and conference calls.

Several issues arose, requiring decisions that affected how the project team conceptualized and phrased exam items. The following points illustrate their decisions:

- Use as little library jargon as possible, and be aware of language issues relating to cultural and ethnic differences and English language proficiency

- When appropriate, create items that address a specific information need or scenario, to provide context;

include academic scenarios of information needs as well as vocational and practical ones, to reflect the diversity of community college students' educational goals and experiences and their personal needs for information

- Use the active voice rather than the passive voice

- Include a mixture of format types, such as multiple-choice and short-answer, matching the format to the outcome assessed; limit the number of answer choices for the multiple-choice items to no more than five; do not use true-false or yes-no answers, because the group agreed that this format is too easy

- Ensure that each item adequately measures the stated outcome

Development of Part A: Cognitive Questions

Each subgroup member was assigned one of the four standards, and he or she wrote test items based on the performance outcomes from the consensus document. It was not entirely clear which outcomes would be excluded from Part A until the group members actually tried to write items, review their work, and revise them. They created two test items for each outcome, so that question variations could be evaluated in the field test. The Part A subgroup, over the course of several drafts and communications, made decisions about which scenarios would be appropriate for a specific outcome and about which outcomes required a format other than multiple choice. Discussions ensued about the merits of designing multiple-choice items with one correct answer versus ones that ask students to "circle all that apply." While it was clear that the "circle all that apply" could be more demanding, there was some concern about scoring them. Exhibit 6.2 illustrates two items which assess the same outcome:

Outcome 1.2.1. Identifies the value and differences of potential resources in a variety of formats (e.g., audiovisual, Web site, book, etc.)

After the consultant reviewed the latest draft, more changes, based on good test design principles, were made, including the following:

- Part A was reorganized so that items of the same format type were grouped together (all the short-answer items, all the multiple-choice items, all the items that include screen shots or boxed text, and so on).

- Within the multiple-choice section, the "circle all that apply" items were grouped separately from the "circle the best answer" items.

Exhibit 6.2. Two Versions of a Test Item Assessing the Same Outcome

Item from Part A, version 1

5. You are training to become a dental hygienist. Which source might offer you the *best* firsthand introduction into a new method of cleaning teeth?
   a. A written manual that comes with some equipment.
   b. A video showing the use of the new equipment.
   c. An in-person demonstration by a dental hygienist.
   d. An encyclopedia article about dental hygiene.

Item from Part A, version 2

8. You want to choose a four-year university to attend. Which source(s) might provide helpful information for you? Circle all that apply.
   a. University catalogue.
   b. University Web site.
   c. Movie about college students.
   d. Interview with a university representative.
   e. *Barron's Guide to Two-Year Colleges*

- A few of the items were revised to improve their clarity.

- The number of negatively phrased items—for example, "Which of the following is NOT an example of a primary source?"—was reduced.

- Consistent shading was used for screen shots and consistent boxes were used for quoted text, and the screen shot or boxed text was always located before the question.

- Some "circle all that apply" items were changed into "select the best answer" ones.

The final step in this phase was production of the Part A answer key and a draft of the scoring rubric for the short-answer items, with the intent that the rubric would be expanded after an analysis of the actual responses to the field test.

Development of Part B: Performance-Based Questions

In the performance portion of the proficiency exam, students would apply knowledge and skills to perform actual tasks instead of selecting correct answers from a list of given responses. The Part B subgroup aimed to produce a set of items that would allow students to demonstrate many of the information competency skills enumerated in the consensus document, "Bay Area Community College Information Competency Standards, Performance Indicators and Outcomes." Specifically, test items required students to perform the following tasks:

- Narrow a broad topic and explain the steps taken to do so

- Pose a research question

- Identify a research question's main concepts and synonyms or related terms

- Do research using three different search tools to identify three relevant information sources for the research question

- Cite each source using a standard citation format

- Describe how each source was found and why it was selected

- Present additional research steps that might be taken to further address the research question

- Evaluate two Web pages according to standard criteria

- Paraphrase main ideas from the information provided on the two Web pages

The performance part was constructed to evaluate a student's abilities to formulate correct and appropriate responses after completing various research steps. Thus, many of the exam questions require an answer, as well as an explanation of how the student arrived at that answer—for example, "Narrow this subject to a manageable topic for the assignment and write the topic down" (Item B.1.a) or "In two or three sentences, describe the steps you took to narrow your topic" (Item B.1.b).

Part B was designed as a Web-based form, to facilitate the capture and sharing of student responses. Although the Part B exam does not adequately assess technological competency—a job more suited to portfolios or project-based assessments—the group felt that it was important for students to demonstrate the basic information technology skills necessary to successfully navigate the on-line format. Initial drafts were more ambitious than the version that finally emerged for the first field test. For example, early versions asked test takers to identify whether a selected source was primary or secondary, popular or scholarly. Although these questions would have covered additional learner outcomes, they were dropped for being too cumbersome, as well as redundant with Part A items.

The full project team discussed at great length to what extent explicit prompts should be added to some Part B items and how detailed they should be. For example, in addition to asking students to describe how they had identified specific resources, should the item include prompts such as "What search tool did you use? What keywords to phrases did you type?" No one wanted to lead test takers, but the team members wanted to clearly inform test takers about what was expected. The group resolved this issue by trying to strike a balance between giving clear instructions that would elicit full responses and keeping the questions sufficiently open-ended to reveal test takers' abilities. As a result, some questions were reworded.

Perhaps the most difficult aspect of developing the Part B items was the conceptualization and development of the scoring rubric. While the subgroup drafted the Part B items, they began a discussion about how to design the scoring rubric. Rubrics are essential for performance-based tasks, because performance assessment does not lend itself to answer keys like multiple-choice tests do. A rubric provides scoring criteria and guidelines so that different people scoring the responses will generally arrive at the same score, thus greatly reducing the subjectivity of scoring. The extent of agreement among different scorers is a measure of the reliability of the assessment instrument.

To prepare for development of the scoring rubric, the subgroup members each completed the exam and constructed a table that mapped test items and responses back to the performance outcomes. In this side-by-side display, performance outcomes were linked with test items and actual responses, and a fourth column was added for inserting ideas about what might go into the scoring rubric. This table formed a preliminary scoring rubric that was used throughout the process of developing the final rubric.

Preparation of the Test Specifications Document

The outline for the test specifications document was prepared during the test development phase, but the final copy was not completed until after the exam went through several revisions and two field tests. The consultant provided guidance and suggestions for the content and organization of this document. Test specifications not only clarify the content and scoring of an instrument but also serve as documentation that allows someone else to modify items or develop new ones yet maintain the integrity of the test design. The test specifications document includes several sections: purpose; description of the content, especially as it relates to the criteria-related levels of performance; details about the development of test items; information about format, administration of the exam, and scoring procedures; charts that map the test items to specific outcomes; and a table that shows the item mix and point values for each standard's outcomes.

Producing the mapping for each standard was a two-step process; each subgroup mapped its items, then a combined mapping was produced, to reflect the entire exam. It cannot be stressed enough how helpful this mapping was; it revealed which outcomes had been inadvertently overlooked in designing test items, and it uncovered which outcomes were represented by multiple items. Table 6.1 illustrates the mapping of several test items to performance outcomes. Table 6.2 provides a further example of this mapping of test items to performance outcomes for Standard One, which states, "The information literate student determines the nature and extent of the information needed."

First Field Test

Table 6.1 illustrates selected items from both parts of the instrument used for the first field test. The first field test sought to identify problematic items, to determine the amount of time required to complete the exam, and to use the actual responses from Part B to help improve the scoring rubric. The cognitive part included thirty-three multiple-choice, five short-answer, and seven matching or ranking items. The performance-based part was composed of seven numbered items, most of which contained subparts. A cover page to Part A also surveyed students about their experience in using libraries

Table 6.1. Selected Items from the Information Competency Proficiency Exam Mapped to Outcomes Assessed

Test Item(s)	Outcome(s) Assessed
Part B.1.a. Your instructor has given you the broad subject "civil rights in America" and an assignment to write a three-to-five-page research paper on some aspect of this topic. Narrow this subject to a manageable topic for the assignment.	1.1.4. Modifies the information need or research question to achieve a manageable focus.
Part A.46. Your research question is: "Do elementary school students receive adequate science instruction in California public schools?" How would you *broaden* this question? Write an example of a broader research question.	
Part B.2. Next, take your narrowed topic and pose it as a research question that you might address in this three-to-five-page writing assignment.	
Part A.2. You need to research an aspect of the topic "education in public schools." Which one of the following would be an appropriate research question? a. Does bilingual education help children attending public schools? b. Should all school children receive free lunches? c. Should states mandate standardized testing for religious schools? d. Do labor unions help teachers keep their jobs?	1.1.2. Formulates appropriate question(s) based on information need or research topic.

Part B.3. You've been given the assignment to write a three-to-five-page research paper on the following topic: "Should colleges be allowed to restrict student speech?" Write in the key concepts represented by the research question.

1.1.5. Identifies key concepts and terms that represent the information need or research topic question.

Part A.4. Which group of keywords *best* describes the information need for the following assignment: "Prepare a presentation about the gains achieved by women in the 1980s."

a. presentation, women, gains
b. women, gains, achieved
c. women, gains, 1980s
d. gains, achieved, 1980s

Part A.25. As you collect sources for your project, it is important to

a. evaluate each source for accuracy and currency
b. print the full text out
c. record all bibliographic information for your Works Cited list
d. answers a. and b.
e. answers a. and c.

2.5.1. Records all pertinent citation information for future reference.

Part B.4.a.1, B.4.b.1, B.4.c.1. Identify three relevant sources for this research question [. . .] a. Write a complete bibliographic citation for the source using the citation format you noted above.

5.3.1. Uses an appropriate documentation style consistently and correctly to cite sources.

Table 6.1. Selected Items from the Information Competency Proficiency Exam Mapped to Outcomes Assessed, *continued*

Test Item(s)	Outcome(s) Assessed
Part A.18. You now own a 1996 Ford Windstar that has given you electrical problems. You need to buy a new car, so you look at the magazine *Consumer Reports*, which says that Windstars have fewer than average electrical repair problems. Which of the following is the *most likely conclusion* to make? a. You should buy another Windstar. b. *Consumer Reports* is wrong. c. You have a different model year from the one described in the report. d. A mechanic damaged your electrical system.	3.3.3. Compares new information with own knowledge and other sources considered authoritative to draw conclusions.
Part B. a.2, b.2, c.2. How did you find the three sources? In two or three sentences, describe your steps, including the search tool(s) used and how you performed your search.	2.1.1. Identifies the types of information contained in a particular system (e.g., types of sources indexed in a particular database/index). 2.2.2. Selects appropriate information retrieval system(s) for a research question/topic based on investigating the scope, content, organization, and help features of such search tools as on-line catalogue, reference sources, periodical databases, Web. 2.2.3. Selects controlled vocabulary specific to the search tool and identifies where controlled vocabulary is used in an item record, and then successfully

searches for additional information using that vocabulary.

2.2.4. Constructs and implements the search strategy, using appropriate search features and commands for the information retrieval system selected (e.g., Boolean logic, truncation, field searching, etc.).

2.3.1. Uses various search systems to retrieve information in a variety of formats, such as on-line library catalogues, reference sources, periodical databases, Web search tools.

Part B.5. In addition to the three sources above, describe in two or three sentences what additional research steps you might take to adequately address the research question.

2.1.3. Identifies other investigative methods to obtain needed information not likely to be available via information retrieval systems (e.g., need to survey or interview experts, etc.).

Part A.20. Copyright protection covers works:

a. as long as the author or creator is still alive.

b. only if an explicit copyright notice (©, or Copyright by . . .) is displayed.

5.1.2. Demonstrates an understanding of intellectual property and copyright laws.

Table 6.1. Selected Items from the Information Competency Proficiency Exam Mapped to Outcomes Assessed, *continued*

Test Item(s)	Outcome(s) Assessed
c. that represent an original idea, regardless of format (text, music, drawing, video . . .). d. only if they have been published.	
Part A.21. You want to use some of the information found in a magazine article for your research paper. Which situation(s) require that you write a footnote citing the source of your information? a. When you copy a whole paragraph. b. When you paraphrase a main point in your own words. c. When you quote a sentence from the article. d. answers a. and c. e. answers a., b., and c.	5.1.3. Defines and identifies examples of plagiarism.

Table 6.2. Exam Items Mapped to Information Competency Outcomes: Standard One

Test Item	Outcome(s) Assessed	Points	Test Section and Item
Which group of keywords best describes the information need for the following assignment: "Prepare a presentation about the gains achieved by women in the 1980s"? (multiple-choice item)	Standard 1. Outcome 1.1.5 Identifies key concepts and terms that represent the information need or research topic question.	1 point	A. 4.
You've been given the assignment to write a three-to-five-page research paper on the following topic: "Should colleges be allowed to restrict student speech?" What are the main concepts for this research question?	Same outcome	9 points Total = 10 points	B. 3. a.1, b.1, c.1

and on-line resources and the amount of their previous training or instruction in research skills; it also asked them for a self-rating of their research skills.

The exam was field-tested in April and May 2002 at four California community colleges in the greater Bay Area, with a sample of twenty-nine students for Part A and nineteen for Part B. The project team did not develop instructions for administering the exam but learned that most of the students completed it in a classroom lab or library setting. Students were given the option of doing both parts or just one part of the exam. Completion time ranged from twenty-five to fifty minutes for Part A and between one hour and one hour and a half for Part B. The sample purposely included nonnative speakers of English and students who did and did not have previous instruction in library research skills. Only a few of the respondents completed both parts of the exam, and because student name or identification number was not required on the separate parts, it was not possible to match them. Three of the project team members scored the completed Part A tests and together compiled comments about problematic items. The Part B subgroup scored the Part B tests and used the responses to further develop the scoring rubric.

Refining Part A

A detailed item analysis, a correlation table, and a report for the Part A results were prepared by the consultant. The item analysis revealed which Part A items were problematic and in need of revision. The correlation table identified which items the higher-scoring students missed and which ones the lower-scoring students missed. The sample was too small to use the factor analysis data or to reliably correlate amount of previous instruction in information competency skills to performance. Based on the consultant's analysis and the project team's, the following activities occurred to improve Part A:

- Several items and answer choices were reworded to improve clarity

- Some items were changed from a multiple-choice to a short-answer format, and vice versa, to adjust the level of difficulty

- A few items were revised to make them more challenging

- A few items were moved to a different section of Part A, to keep item types together

- "Circle all that apply" choices were eliminated

- The services of a secretary were used to improve the look of Part A

Another concern was the desire to establish empirically a valid cutoff score for passing the exam. From various approaches suggested by the consultant, the project team chose a "panel of experts" approach. As it turned out, this approach was used only for Part A items. Three members of the Part A subgroup estimated the percentage of students that could answer each individual question correctly and later compared these estimates to the actual percentage of students who correctly answered each item. The consultant suggested that the estimated percentages might be averaged to arrive at a cutoff score. As it turned out, the sample was not large enough to reliably use these calculations to establish a cutoff score.

Developing the Part B Scoring Rubric

Development of the Part B scoring rubric involved many steps. Initially, a three-level scoring rubric was developed, with exemplary, competent, and emergent performance levels. Discussions about these distinctions were critical to decisions about performance levels. Despite these efforts, after the consultant and another project team member reviewed the first draft of the rubric and attempted to use it to score a couple of completed tests, the three-level scoring concept was dropped. The three-level scoring system, while it might be useful in a course or another assessment setting, was not deemed suitable for the project's purpose of a challenge-out test, which needs to set a standard, showing whether the performance bar has been met or not.

There were nineteen Part B submissions from the first field test, and these provided the substance both for devising the scoring rubric and for pretesting it. In essence, a process of deconstruction was applied: if both reader and author were autonomous, then what meanings were actually in the responses, and what did they signify? How could discrete and describable criteria be enumerated so that levels of correctness could be identified? And what levels of performance should be expected? That is, where was the bar defining performance that reflected the level of information competence appropriate for two-year college graduates?

One of the most challenging tasks was to devise language to describe the elements distinguishing the meaning of an adequate response. For example, most scorers would correctly recognize a research topic that has been sufficiently narrowed to be appropriate for a three-to-five-page research paper, but coming up with a description of what characterizes a sufficiently narrowed research topic that could be applied across research questions was another matter. In analyzing student responses, the important questions were these: If someone responded adequately or well on an item, what specific characteristics were associated with that response? For test responses that obviously failed to hit the mark, what characterized those responses and others like them? The goal was to extract these characteristics and describe them generically, so that any librarian-scorer could apply them. For example, the criteria for scoring whether a student has developed an appropriately narrowed topic (Item B.1.a) reads, in part, "1. The topic is narrowed by specifying time frame, or persons, or organization or group, or location, or event or incident, or some combination of these, or other similar, appropriate limiter(s) is (are) applied." Some test items and their performance outcomes were more complex and composed of subparts; the team had to address not only the level of performance required for competency on each subpart but also the issue of which competencies had to be demonstrated in tandem.

Working independently and using the evolving rubric, subgroup members scored tests, compared scores, and discussed how specific scores had been determined. Developing and refining the scoring rubric required many iterations. As a last step in finalizing the rubric before using it in the second field test, the subgroup added examples of adequate and inadequate responses to clarify the meaning of the criteria and assigned a weighted scale of numerical values for scoring.

Second Field Test

The summer months of 2002 provided some time and some distance from the project, allowing the team to reflect on the findings of the first field test. For the Part B subgroup, the time was used to refine the scoring rubric and other supporting documentation for Part B. Table 6.3 is an extract from the scoring rubric that was used for the second field test. Project team members decided to weight the scores, in order to have a total of 100 possible points. For most test items, all of the criteria had to be satisfied in order for the student to score any points; partial fulfillment of the criteria, with a corresponding score, was allowed on only three of the items.

The preparations for the second field test involved much planning and the production of instructions and other documentation. The Part B subgroup finalized the scoring rubric and three other supporting documents: "Introductory Notes on the Performance Exam and Scoring," a scoring manual, and a scoring sheet. The Part A subgroup completed the scoring rubric for the short-answer items on Part A and a combined answer key and scoring sheet.

The entire project team participated in a telephone conference call in which the details and issues of administering and scoring the exam were finalized. For the second field test, the group invited additional institutions, to ensure that a sample of at least fifty respondents would complete the entire exam. Another goal was to test the accuracy and usability of the newly developed scoring rubrics by asking librarians not previously associated with this project to use them.

Administration of the Second Field Test

A packet of materials was distributed both electronically and by postal mail to the six participating community colleges in early November 2002, so that the exam could be administered before the

Table 6.3. Example from Scoring Rubric for Part B Performance Items

Test Item	Criteria to Apply	What Constitutes Competent	Notes on Scoring	Score and Weighted Score
Item B. 1a. Your instructor has given you the broad topic "civil rights in America" and an assignment to write a three-to-five-page research paper on some aspect of this topic. Narrow this to a manageable topic for the assignment.	Criterion 1: Topic is narrowed by specifying time frame, or persons, or organization or group, or location, or event or incident, or some combination of these, or other similar appropriate limiter(s) is (are) applied. AND Criterion 2: Narrowed topic is within subject assigned.	At least one of the narrowing techniques has been applied to the subject AND The other two criteria are met.	Broad topic is "civil rights in America." *Examples of appropriately narrowed topics:* • "status of Arab-American civil rights after September 11, 2001" (narrowed by time frame and group) • "effects of the University of California system prohibiting race-based admissions criteria" (narrowed by organization and event) *Example of topic not properly narrowed:* • "civil rights movement in America: equality then and now" (no time period, incident, or group to focus)	Criterion 1 = 1 Criterion 2 = 1 Criterion 3 = 1 3 out of 3 = 1 0, 1 or 2 out of 3 = 0 Possible scores: 0, 1 **Weighted score:** 1 = 8 0 = 0

AND

Criterion 3:
Narrowed topic is appropriate to a three-to-five-page research paper.

Example of topic not within assigned subject:
- "two sides fighting the Civil War"

Example of topic too broad:
- "Black Americans' civil rights"

| **Item B. 5.** In addition to the three sources you've selected, describe in two or three sentences at least two additional research steps you might take to adequately address the research question. | Student presents at least two possible and plausible steps to revise the search strategy by identifying other investigative methods or retrieval systems, and/or type of sources on the topic. | *Examples of appropriate responses:*
 • "Ask a librarian or a professor of law. Identify additional keywords or subjects to use in searches"
 • "Visit several campuses and interview newspaper writers, as well as search through back issues of campus newspapers." | Each possible and plausible research step = 1

 2 out of 2 = 1

 0, 1, or 2 = 0

 Possible scores: 0, 1 |
| | The criterion is met. | *Examples of inadequate responses:*
 • "Try the catalogue."
 • "Go in person to another library, or watch a good news program." | **Weighted score:**
 1 = 8
 0 = 0 |

end of the fall semester. This packet contained a cover letter detailing how to administer and score the exam; Parts A and B of the exam; scoring sheets and instructions; Part A answer key; and Part B scoring manual and instructions for using the scoring rubric. Five of the six participating institutions used the exam in the context of an information competency class, which provided an actual test-taking environment. The other institution posted a sign in the library with an enticement of a $5.00 copy card. To encourage timely return of the completed tests and reduce the burden of using class time, the instructions for administering the exam stipulated that students should complete the paper copy of Part A in a classroom setting but were allowed to complete the on-line Part B at home or in another setting where they had Internet access. Deadlines were established for the completion of Part B by each of the librarians who administered the exam.

Participating librarians were asked to score both parts of each exam taken by students at their institution and return them by the end of January 2003. In order to assess interrater reliability, each Part B was also scored by two project team members; thus, each completed Part B was scored by three individuals. The short-answer items on Part A were also scored by one other project team member, in order to evaluate agreement of scorers using the Part A answer key.

The receipt and coordination of the completed Part B's was a bit demanding, because it involved the redistribution of the completed Part B's to two other scorers. One project team member handled this task, tracking the receipt and redistribution of the Part B's by using the student's test identification number, which was the last four digits of the social security number plus a college code. She also acted as a clearinghouse for the completed Part B's, which were submitted in sections by some students, resulting in two or three submissions by a student. She was also able to notice incomplete Part B's and alert another team member who was coordinating the receipt of the completed Part A's. A conversation between these two team members clarified the definition of an incomplete Part B, which would not be used in the data analysis.

The Part B clearinghouse team member also developed a table that recorded the item-by-item scores from each of the three librarian-scorers. Midway through the Part B scoring process, she became aware of a fairly large range of scores among the three librarian-scorers for certain items and suggested a phone conference to clarify the use and interpretation of the scoring rubric. The phone conference allowed each of the scorers to describe his or her interpretation of the respondents' answers and made it clearer which aspects each scorer had focused on. As a result of the phone conference, project team members recorded observations for the revision of the rubric and for scorer training. To preserve the integrity of the second field test, no scores were changed, and the rubric remained as it was for the completion of the second field test. The project team began to articulate the idea that each institution using this exam might need to develop its own perspective on how to evaluate and score the range of answers, depending on its information competency instructional program. The major observation that came from the phone conference was that not enough attention had been devoted to training the scorers to use the rubric.

The Part A exams and scoring sheets were mailed to another project team member, who reviewed all submissions in order to match the students' identification numbers with those on the list of completed Part B exams. After matching the test takers' identification numbers for both parts, she compiled for the consultant's analysis six packets of completed scoring sheets and supporting documentation, one for each institution. While there were many more submissions, Table 6.4 shows the originating institutions for the fifty-seven completed exams included in the analysis.

Findings from the Second Field Test

Findings from the second field test came from the consultant's analysis as well as from the experiences and reflections of the project team members and participating librarians. The consultant had been asked to provide overall descriptive statistics; item analyses from both parts of the exam; data on correlation of overall performance with students'

Table 6.4. Original Institutions Completing the Exams

Institution	Number of Exams	Percentage of Total
City College of San Francisco	12	21.1%
Diablo Valley College	11	19.3
Foothill College	4	7.0
Glendale Community College	19	33.3
San Joaquin Delta College	5	8.7
Santa Rosa Junior College	6	10.6
Total	57	100%

self-assessment of their research skills and with their response to a survey question about previous instruction in doing library or Web research; and an analysis of the relationship between scores on Part A and Part B. The consultant's overall analysis found that the instrument needed some further work, a finding that confirmed much of the project team's own observations derived from the scoring process. Selected findings from the consultant's descriptive statistics and item analysis follow:

- Part A's reliability score of .76 on the Kuder-Richardson 20 scale was not sufficiently high. Eight items in need of revision were identified.

- Interrater reliability on Part A was .99, which means that the answer key and rubric worked well for the eight short-answer items.

- Part A scores ranged from 61 high (out of 64 unweighted points possible) to 21 low. Mean score was 45.2 points (SD = 8.57), and the median score was 45 points. Thirty-one students scored 45 or higher, which is 54.4 percent of the total number of fifty-seven students; a score of 45 or higher reflects 70.3 percent of the items correct. Eighteen students (31.6 percent of the total) scored 51 or higher, reflecting 80 percent or more of the items correct.

- Interrater reliability on Part B was .71-.77, which is insufficient for overall test score reliability.

- On Part B, averaging the three scores for each test, the range was from 90.3 high to 11.3 low. Mean score of the three scorers' totals was 51.4 points out of a possible 100 weighted points (SD = 18.43), and the median score was 47.3.

- The relationship between how students rate their information literacy skills and their actual performance was not very strong (for Part A, rho = .275, $p < .04$, and for Part B, rho = .10, $p. < 04$), but the mean self-rating was 7.1 on a 10-point scale, with 10 as the highest score.

- A positive and fairly high correlation was found between the total score on Part A and the total score on Part B (rho = .588, $p < .0001$).

- Because of multiple responses to the survey item asking about previous library skills instruction, only descriptive statistics were generated. For Part A, for the thirty-one students (57.4 percent) who indicated that they had completed either a credit course or some combination of instruction (for example, credit course plus library workshop; credit course plus workshop plus college class presentation; or workshop plus college class presentation plus high school class presentation), the mean score was 42.25 (out of 64 possible points). For the eleven students (20.4 percent) who indicated that they had had only a single past instructional experience (for example, only a library workshop or only a class presentation), the mean score was 39.45. The

remaining respondents did not respond to this item.
For Part B, the same thirty-one students who had completed a credit course or some combination of instruction earned a mean score of 53.9, while the eleven
students with a single instructional experience earned a
mean score of 44.9. Significance tests were not com-
puted, but it seems that the scores for those who had
either a credit course or some combination of instructional offerings were a bit higher than those students
who had had only one instructional offering.

- Findings revealed that it was not possible to use a student's score on Part A or Part B to predict his or her
  performance on the other part of the exam.

Final Revision of the Exam

Absorbing the consultant's report and deciding how to complete
the project required a great deal of study and discussion. The project team had several e-mail exchanges, two phone conferences, and
an all-day meeting to analyze the consultant's report and make plans
for how to address the findings and complete the project. They used
the summer months of 2003 to carry out the decisions reached during these various conversations. They decided not to conduct a
third field test, partly because of time constraints but primarily
because team members were convinced that use of the instrument
would likely result in some modifications to adapt it for each individual institution. They felt that a better contribution would be
made by using the findings from the second field test to revise the
problem items in both parts and the scoring rubric for Part B, as well
as preparing a more detailed explanation of why and how items
were developed. In addition to the revision activities, the team's
goal included the preparation of thorough documentation to ensure
that good test design practices would be followed when others customized the instrument for their local needs. All the team members

agreed that the final report would need to include a caveat or two about the exam's lack of statistical reliability and validity, since the revisions would not be further field-tested.

The final revision of the instrument benefited from several inputs. One input came during an all-day meeting of the project team members, when another examination of the content validity of test items was made by reviewing the mapping of test items to performance outcomes. As a result, the maps were slightly revised and a few Part A test items were identified for revision in order to improve the fit between the outcome and the item. Another input came from the consultant's item analysis, which flagged items that the better-performing students had missed. These items were examined to ensure that they were clearly phrased and not misleading. In some cases, the items were rephrased or completely redesigned; in others the project team decided that it was an appropriately difficult item and did not need revision. A third input came from an ESL instructor's examination of both parts of the exam. Her involvement was requested by one of the project team members after the draft instrument was shared with a large group of faculty. Faculty comments identified possible difficulties for nonnative speakers of English in some items. Several items were rewritten to simplify and clarify the language for nonnative speakers of English.

Part B items also benefited from the three inputs discussed above; they were also carefully reviewed and revised as needed. The major issues for Part B revision centered on finding ways to encourage students to write more complete explanations of their research steps and reasons for their responses as well as increasing the interrater reliability for scoring. Several items were slightly revised to provide more prompts for students. The scoring rubric was improved by including many more examples of adequate and inadequate student responses, as well as more notes to the scorer. Moreover, suggestions were made in the documentation about conducting training for the scorers before using the rubric. In addition to issues of ensuring content validity, unintentional weighting of certain outcomes over others concerned the team members. They looked at the combined point totals and identified some outcomes that were mapped to two or more test items. The point of this activity was to more consciously decide whether they wanted to weight certain outcomes more heavily than others. For example, they discovered that the outcomes associated with posing and modifying a research question and identifying the major concepts in the research question, as well as keywords and synonyms, represented a larger proportion of points than they felt appropriate. As a result of this activity, two items were eliminated from Part A, a new item was added, and the assignment of weighted points in Part B was revised.

Scoring Options

The project team also had a phone conference dedicated to the rationale behind the allocation of weighting for items in Part B and the overall scoring of the exam. They dismissed the idea of trying to change the scoring so that each part of the exam had the same amount of points, since there was agreement about not wanting to assign more than one point for each of Part A's multiple-choice and matching items. Consensus also supported the higher possible points for Part B, since the performance-based part was felt to be more challenging and indicative of overall information competency. Thus, the final instrument includes two parts with total possible points allocated as follows: Part A has 60 points, and Part B has 100 points. Team members also discussed the notion that a passing score for a challenge-out exam should probably not be higher than the C-level performance expected of students in typical information competency credit courses. Recognizing that views on this issue would most likely vary among individual institutions, they decided to present several scoring options so that each institution could select one that was appropriate. The three options are as follows:

1. A passing score could be expressed in total points from both parts of the exam that are necessary to pass. One can easily

calculate a percentage of correct answers for both parts of the exam by setting the total possible points equal to 100 percent. *Example:* Total possible points = 160 – 100 percent; passing score is decided to be 70 percent. A student would need to score 112 total points or more in order to pass the exam. This option allows a student to compensate for poor performance in one part with better performance in the other part.

Variation of Option 1: The score for Part A is changed to a percentage. Part B is already 100 points, so it is easily converted to a percentage. The two percentages are added together and divided by two which becomes the "final score." A threshold is established for a passing grade. *Example:* A student could score 32 on Part A (50 percent of the items correct) and 100 percent on Part B; the average would be 75 percent, a passing score if the threshold is 70 percent.

2. A passing score is established for each part of the exam. Each part maintains the same threshold (for example, 70 percent). In this scenario, a student has to perform at a passing level on each part in order to pass the whole exam.

3. A passing score or percentage is established for each part of the exam, but in this case one part could be different than the other (for example, 70 percent for Part A and 80 percent for Part B). In this scenario, a student has to perform at a passing level on each part, but one part could be weighted more heavily.

Final Products

The final stage of the project involved another lengthy conversation among the project team members to review the final revisions of the exam and scoring rubric, as well as the documentation about the development of test items. As part of this final review, they reached consensus about the rewording of Part A and Part B items as well as the detailed explanation about how the items were developed.

They also decided to change the weighting of the Part B items so that the weighted points assigned to the three major sections would be more equivalent.

Finally, in October 2003, all the project's products were completed and posted to the project's Web page. At http://www.topsy.org, readers will find a link entitled "Bay Area Community Colleges Information Competency Assessment Project," which leads to the following documents:

- Final report

- Consensus standards document, "Bay Area Community College Information Competency Standards, Performance Indicators and Outcomes," which was used for developing the exam items

- Test specifications document, which includes explanations about the development of exam items and advice on making modifications for local use

- Mappings of exam items to performance outcomes for each of the information literacy standards that the instrument assesses

- The latest versions of Part A and Part B, with revised scoring rubrics and most of the supporting documentation that was used to administer the instrument in the second field test

Dissemination of Project Activities and Findings

There were several informal and formal opportunities to share information about the project and the results of the two field tests over the course of this three-year project:

- Informal sharing of information with library and discipline-based faculty colleagues on the community college campuses of each of the project team's members

- Frequent sharing of drafts and ideas via e-mail and phone conferences among members within both subgroups, between the two subgroups of the project team, and with external colleagues for observations and reactions

- Periodic project updates to a contact person at a neighboring California State University

- Presentations at four conferences—the Pre-conference on Information Literacy at the annual California Community Colleges Chancellor's Office Conference (March 2002); the California Academic and Research Libraries (CARL) annual conference (May 2002); the California Library Association Conference, Academic Libraries section program (November 2002); and the ACRL national conference (April 2003)—and at two California Community College library workshops (March 2003)

- A progress report and a final report published in the *CARL Newsletter* (September 2002 and September 2003)

- Project documents and sample test items published on the Web site of one of the project team members (http://www.topsy.org)

- Postings to California academic library and national library instruction and information competency listservs about the existence of the exam and supporting documentation at the project Web site

Collaboration with the California State University (CSU) librarians was expanded midway through the project. Quite fortuitously, the manager for the information competence initiative from the CSU system's Office of the Chancellor made contact with a member of the project team. Thanks to her interest and initiative, early drafts of test items were shared with the CSU Information Competence Test Development Task Force. This group of CSU librarians was involved in a task similar to ours. A productive meeting between the two groups was held in spring 2002, which resulted in an improved understanding of our respective purposes and a commitment to continue to share all drafts and results of our work. We had opportunities at two other times to meet with the CSU system contact person, a representative from our project, and contacts from an Association for Research Libraries–affiliated project, Project SAILS. (Project SAILS, which began after our Bay Area Community College Information Competence Assessment Project, is a large-scale project dedicated to developing a standardized information literacy assessment instrument.) These meetings were held at the American Library Association midwinter meeting in January 2003 and at the ACRL national conference in April 2003.

Dissemination of information on our project was greatly enhanced during the first field test in April 2002 by posting on the project Web site of several digital documents: Part B of the exam, the scoring rubric, and some introductory information about the project and the exam. During the time that Part B was on the Web site, several librarians made inquiries about the project. Some asked for permission to use Part B of the exam and inquired about the timeline for a final instrument. After the first field test, Part B was removed from the Web site; however, copies of both parts of the exam were made available to all interested parties who personally contacted a project member.

Information sharing expanded again with the second field test. From the initial four institutions who participated in the first field test, the number grew to eight institutions with whom information was shared and to whom an invitation to participate was extended. While the final number of institutions who participated was six, several others became better informed about this project. In addition, after one of the project team members made a presentation at the California Library Association conference in November 2002, interested attendees were sent background information and copies of the documents for the second field test, even though they were unable to participate.

By the end of the project in fall 2003, all the supporting documentation and revised versions of both parts of the instrument had been posted at the project's Web site, with an invitation for any library to use or modify the exam for their own purposes. Certain courtesies are requested; for example, those who use or modify the exam are asked to use the explanatory information and advice for implementation. In addition, they are asked to share their results and their experiences with using the instrument. The project team plans to leave these digital materials on the project Web page at least through 2004. The idea is to share not only the project's "final" instrument but also the how-to information, so that others can modify the exam for their own purposes yet maintain the integrity of the exam items in terms of good test design.

Lessons Learned and Next Steps

This three-year undertaking was a remarkable example of dedicated librarian collaboration and commitment to seeing a project succeed. While not interdisciplinary in the traditional sense, it was certainly intersegmental and interinstitutional. Operating on a shoestring, all the project team librarians spent endless hours of their own time, although they had some support from their respective institutions. A collegial model of interacting became the norm, though each subgroup had a primary mover or movers. At various times during the project, one of the team members assumed a coordinating role because of her proximity to the consultant. Undoubtedly, what helped the project succeed was identifying a clear purpose from the start; the team members' experience and expertise in teaching and assessing information competency skills; the small size of the team; and the division into two working subgroups to get things done. Ongoing dissemination of information and feedback aided this project tremendously by helping team members become clearer about tasks and objectives, as well as gain encouragement from others.

The project team learned that a regional approach to a common need is a viable one that can succeed, even with a fairly large and complex project. In the interest of learning from the team's experiences, the following suggestions are offered:

- Prepare a very detailed project plan and timeline in the early stages so that the complexity and length of time required for the project phases can be anticipated

- Secure a large enough grant that you can hire the consultant at the very beginning, so that he or she can guide the development of the test specifications document and the exam items early in the process

- Hire production help for preparation of the exam and supporting documents, and especially for putting both on-line

- Use more institutions than our project team did for the first field test, in order to have a large sample; give specific instructions on how to administer it, to ensure that most students complete both parts of the exam

- Consciously plan ways to recruit students who have been exposed to a range of previous instruction—for example, none, workshops only, an information competency class

- Plan incentives for students to complete the exam, to maximize the number of test takers from each institution

- Designate a team member to coordinate the various tasks and to be responsible for ensuring timely communication between the working subgroups

- Use the combined mapping of test items from both parts of the exam as a tool for deciding on the weighting of points and possible elimination of test items

- Dedicate time to training the scorers to use the rubric for the performance-based part

For community colleges that plan to use the proficiency exam as a challenge-out or credit-by-exam option for an information competency requirement, there is still work to be done. Librarians will need to work with their testing office or faculty testing committee to have the exam approved and to address issues related to official record keeping for transcript purposes. This step must involve other faculty and academic staff, in order to review and possibly modify the exam for local use.

Librarians who decide to use the exam, or part of it, for course assessment purposes might want to collaborate with course instructors to modify the exam so that specific performance outcomes related to the use of information (Standard Four) can be included. For example, if an institution decides to assess all the performance outcomes related to information competency within an English or speech course, the exam could be combined with an assessment of writing or speaking assignments collected in a portfolio.

The project team members are satisfied with the results of this project, and even though the original goal of developing a scientifically valid and reliable instrument was not totally fulfilled, they feel that the detailed documentation about how the exam items were developed and scored will be useful for replication and modification by individual schools.

Notes

1. For detailed information about the chronology of these initiatives and text of these various reports and resolutions, see http://www. topsy.org/infocomp.html.

2. The initial project team included these Bay Area librarians: Bonnie Gratch-Lindauer and Brian Lym, City College of San Francisco; Amelie Brown and Andy Kivel, Diablo Valley College; Micca Gray, Santa Rosa Junior College; Topsy Smalley, Cabrillo College; and Pam Baker, CSU Monterey Bay. Active contributors were Evelyn Posamentier, Skyline College; Jun Wang, Delta College; and Karen Gillette, Foothill College. We thank all of these institutions for their support. The project team acknowledges CARL for the research grant award and DVC for grant monies donated for consulting fees. They owe a huge debt of gratitude to team member Topsy Smalley for posting and maintaining the project documents on her Web site, http://www.topsy.org.

3. See http://www.topsy.org for the complete consensus document.

References

Association of College and Research Libraries. *Information Literacy Competency Standards for Higher Education.* Chicago: Association of College and Research Libraries, 2000. Also available at http://www.ala.org/Content/ NavigationMenu/ACRL/Standards. http://www.ala.org/Content/ NavigationMenu/ACRL/Standards_and_Guidelines/Information_ Literacy_Competency_Standards_for_Higher_Education.htm.

Association of College and Research Libraries. "Objectives for Information Literacy Instruction: A Model Statement for Academic Librarians" 2001. http://www.ala.org/Content/NavigationMenu/ACRL/Standards_and_ Guidelines/Objectives_for_Information_Literacy_Instruction__A_ Model_Statement_for_Academic_Librarians.htm.

7

Assessing Information Literacy

Lynn Cameron

Many librarians feel unprepared to conduct an assessment of information literacy. We often do not know where to begin and may not have anyone at our institution with the time or expertise to help us. Yet assessment can offer an opportunity for librarians and teaching faculty to develop learning objectives for information literacy, plan instruction that is an integral part of the curriculum, and construct instruments that measure the stated objectives. We can use test results to identify weak areas of skill, determine the efficacy of an instruction program, and make improvements. In the past, we often measured the success of an instruction program by the number of students or classes instructed. Assessment offers us a chance to go beyond counting sessions and students and show that students have actually learned the skills they need to complete their assignments and become independent learners. The question is no longer "Are we reaching students through our instruction program?" The question is now "Are students demonstrating that they have learned information literacy skills?"

In the 1980s, when higher education was being called upon for greater accountability, librarians searched fruitlessly for models for assessing what we then called library skills. With limited resources available, librarians at James Madison University (JMU), in collaboration with faculty and assessment specialists, started small and developed our own instrument: the Library Skills Test, a paper-and-pencil, multiple-choice assessment for students in general education. We administered this test, or revised versions of it, to thousands of students over a period of several years. Our main goal was to assess the library instruction program. By the late 1990s, our efforts had evolved. We began using the on-line Information-Seeking Skills Test (ISST) as a competency test that all students were required to pass by the end of their first year. Our goal had changed from assessing our instruction program to holding every student accountable for learning important skills. In addition to the general education assessment, JMU assessed the information literacy of seniors in more than fifteen different majors, using locally developed instruments that focused on skills specific to each discipline. This chapter will take a close and candid look at these efforts, with special attention to their success in measuring student learning and improving instruction.

Instruction Program Assessment

The impetus for assessment in Virginia originated in the mid-1980s, when the Virginia State Council of Higher Education mandated that each state-supported institution have an assessment plan for general education and the majors. The council later instituted a technology core competency requirement but left it up to the individual schools to define and implement the requirement. Librarians across the state advocated defining this requirement to include information literacy.

JMU created the Office of Student Assessment to coordinate assessment of educational outcomes for compliance with Virginia State Council of Higher Education guidelines and Southern Association of Colleges and Schools criteria. At JMU, assessment is an ongoing process oriented toward improvement. All students and programs participate. Assessment of educational programs is reported through an academic program review process, conducted in five-year cycles.

Efforts to assess information literacy began at JMU in 1989, when the university invited academic departments and other units to assess whether educational goals were being achieved. To help support this effort, the university designated two annual institutional assessment days for administering tests. One, integrated into freshman orientation in August, was to gather baseline information on entering first-year students. The other, held in February, was for both general education and the majors. Classes were canceled, and students were required to participate. The library was invited to develop an assessment test to measure library skills, long considered an essential part of an undergraduate education.

The library had a long-standing library instruction program that reached about ten thousand students a year. The two-tiered program consisted of a self-paced workbook to be completed by all first-year students taking English 101 and 102, and course-related instruction offered to majors by librarians, who served as liaisons with academic departments.

The possibility of being involved in assessment, though a little daunting, was very appealing. The library had been investing a large amount of resources in its instruction program, yet we had little evidence of its effectiveness, aside from appreciative letters from faculty and some anecdotal evidence. Assessing students' skills would tell us whether our use of resources was justified. In addition, we saw an opportunity to survey student attitudes and experiences relating to library services, collections, and methods of instruction. The Office of Student Assessment, staffed by professional assessment specialists, offered to guide us through the steps of development, administration, and interpretation of the test.

The first step in planning our assessment was to decide what our learning objectives were and whom we would test. We identified five objectives: (1) to measure whether JMU students have mastered the essential library skills; (2) to examine students' attitudes that affect library use; (3) to evaluate the effectiveness of the instructional program; (4) to determine the degree to which JMU students are required to use the library in their courses; and (5) to gather information on the frequency and nature of students' use of the library. We wanted to evaluate entering freshmen, second-semester sophomores, and seniors in the majors. Assessing students at these three levels would provide us a good picture of student learning over the full four years. We began by testing sophomores on February Assessment Day to determine the skills they had retained from the first year. The following year, we tested new freshmen on August Assessment Day to see what they knew on entering JMU. Comparative data for beginning freshmen and sophomores would reveal the effectiveness of the workbook as a teaching tool and would help to identify areas of the curriculum that needed strengthening.

Blueprint for the Library Skills Test

Taking into account the content of our library workbook and the skills we emphasized in course-related instruction, we developed a test blueprint for our instrument. (A test blueprint identifies areas to be tested and determines the relative weight of each area.) Our test blueprint targeted four areas: (1) basic reference skills; (2) LEO, the on-line catalogue; (3) search strategy; and (4) library services. The relative weight for each is as follows:

Basic reference skills	17 items
LEO, the on-line catalogue	9 items
Search strategy	3 items
Library services	4 items
Total	33 items

Developing a Reliable Instrument

With blueprint in hand, we began writing multiple-choice items. Our goal was to have a mix of easy, moderate, and difficult items. On this early test, we wrote items that required students to know specific reference tools, such as *Statistical Abstract of the United States*,

Library of Congress Subject Headings, and *Reader's Guide to Periodical Literature*. In later years, we decided that it is more important for students to know general concepts, employ effective search strategies, and evaluate the quality of sources than to know specific reference tools, which may change over time. Several librarians contributed questions to the Library Skills Test. It was helpful to have multiple points of view, both for writing the questions and for critical responses to new items.

After the items were written and reviewed by library colleagues and English faculty, we conducted pilot testing in several classes made available by the English faculty. On the basis of student responses, we made improvements to the test. We found that some of our questions used library jargon that was not familiar to students. Using terminology that could be clearly understood proved to be a real challenge. The pilot test exposed several problems that we had been unable to anticipate. If everybody answers a question right, it may be too easy. If everybody misses it, it may be too hard. If a large percentage chooses the same wrong answer, the item may be confusing, or the students may just need to learn the right answer.

Once we completed pilot testing, the assessment specialists analyzed the data for reliability—the consistency with which the test is measuring the intended construct. One method that estimates the internal consistency of test items is calculating Cronbach's alpha. The test scores are divided into high performers, low performers, and middle performers. If the high performers score better on a given question than the low performers, then that question is discriminating well, or working consistently with the other items. On the other hand, if the low performers score better on a given item than the high performers, there may be a problem. Fixing problematic items usually improves reliability. The first time we administered the test on an assessment day, the Cronbach's alpha was in the range of .69, which is quite adequate for program evaluation purposes. (Cronbach's alpha ranges from 0 to 1, with 1 being the highest consistency.) Increasing the total number of items usually has a strong positive effect on reliability. The following year we increased the number of questions from thirty-three to forty-seven, and the reliability jumped to .77—a significant improvement.

Developing Survey Questions

In addition to the test questions that measured students' knowledge and skills, we added a separate section of survey items on attitudes and experiences:

- Methods and experiences contributing to ways students learn to use the library (8 items)

- Personal attitudes about the library (7 items)

- Frequency of library use for various purposes (10 items)

- Estimation of the proportion of courses that require student use of the library (1 item)

- Level of comfort with the on-line catalogue and technology in general (5 items)

To survey attitudes about instructional interventions, we asked how helpful students found the freshman *Library Skills Workbook* (Cameron, 1987), course-related instruction, individual assistance, and learning on their own. Students could choose "Have not used," "Not helpful at all," "Not very helpful," "Helpful," and "Very helpful." We also asked how frequently they use the on-line catalogue and CD-ROMs and how comfortable they feel with technology. We asked them to rate their level of apprehension and their level of confidence when asked to find information in the library. We asked what portion of their courses required them to use the library to find information, excluding reserves. We asked how frequently they use various collections—for example government documents. All this information, in conjunction with test performance, was intended to give us a good picture of students' use of the library at JMU.

Setting Expectations for Performance

Before administering the test, librarians set expectations on student performance on the thirty-three-item test to establish a threshold for competent library use. We decided students would need to get twenty-one items correct to be minimally competent. The expectations for performance for each level of competence are shown below.

Level of Competence	Expected Score
Exceptionally competent	32–33
Competent	25–31
Minimally competent	21–24
Incompetent	0–20

Administering the Test

The newly revised test, composed of thirty-three test questions and thirty-one survey items, was administered to 317 sophomores on February Assessment Day in 1990. The Center For Assessment and Research Studies generated a random sample from the student information system. The university administration sent letters to these students requiring them to take the Library Skills Test. Faculty promoted participation in class. Having the Center for Assessment and Research Studies take full responsibility for making copies of the test, scheduling rooms for administration, inviting students to come, and proctoring the test made Assessment Day flow smoothly with minimal involvement on the part of the library.

Test Results

Assessment results proved useful. They helped us develop a better understanding of student knowledge, experiences, and attitudes. Findings confirmed that JMU students were acquiring essential library skills by the second semester of their sophomore year. Ninety percent of the students made a score that showed some degree of competence on the total test. Students performed best on library services and search strategy. They had the greatest difficulty with questions about LEO, the on-line catalogue, with 24 percent making an incompetent score on that portion of the test. Table 7.1 shows how well they performed in each area outlined by the blueprint and on the total test.

Poor performance on questions relating to the on-line catalogue captured the attention of the library administration. Was the students' lack of knowledge the problem, or was it the catalogue software, which was not particularly user-friendly? These results were used to make a compelling case for migrating to a new system. The Virginia State Council of Higher Education praised JMU for making decisions based on assessment results.

Student performance on individual test items and in blueprint areas revealed gaps in their learning. We strengthened our coverage of these areas in the workbook to address weaknesses.

Table 7.1. Student Performance on Library Skills Test, by Area, February 1990

	Percentage			
Area	Exceptionally Competent	Competent	Minimally Competent	Incompetent
Basic reference skills	12	47	31	9
LEO library catalogue	5	46	25	24
Search strategies	67	27	0	6
Familiarity with services	62	29	0	9
Total test	1	61	28	10

Survey Results

The results of the survey questions were fascinating. Students were asked whether they had experienced several different methods of instruction and how useful they found each. The results are shown in Table 7.2. Students from this administration of the test showed a definite preference for individual assistance from a librarian, help from classmates, the *Library Skills Workbook*, and library handouts. Course-related instruction by professors ranked last and course-related instruction by librarians, next to last.

We were surprised that nearly a third of the students had not used the workbook. Some could have been transfers or students who skipped English 101 and 102 through advanced placement. We had no idea that such a large portion of students was missing instruction during the first year. Of the students who did complete the workbook, we were pleased that 81 percent found it to be "useful" or "very useful." This was a powerful affirmation of the workbook as an effective teaching tool, at least as viewed by students. The English

Table 7.2. Student Ratings of Instructional Methods

Source for Learning Library Skill	Percentage Who Never Used the Skill	Percentage Who Found the Skill Useful or Very Useful
Assistance from librarian	17	85
Help from classmates	11	85
Library Skills Workbook	32	81
Library handouts	27	71
Learned before coming to JMU	33	68
Librarian instructing class	59	54
Professor instructing class	46	47

Department vowed to tighten the loopholes that allowed students to progress to the sophomore year without completing the workbook.

Nearly a third of the students who were tested reported that they had not learned library skills before coming to JMU. Virginia public schools had *Standards of Learning Objectives for Virginia Public Schools: Library/Information Use* (Virginia Department of Education, 1986) in place at the time. Students either were not taught to use the library or did not feel that their library learning experiences were substantive enough to report. This lack of training prior to college is surprising, given the highly select student body at JMU.

Results for instructional methods were interesting, but not conclusive. Library learning appears to be gained from a number of interrelated sources. As a result of this assessment, we wanted to learn more about the effectiveness of course-related instruction by librarians, which is a major component of our instruction program. The preferred sources of learning—the workbook, help from classmates or librarians, learning on their own, and using printed handouts—are all interactive or individualized. On the other hand, listening to a presentation in the classroom can be a passive experience. These findings had implications for the design of course-related instruction by liaison librarians. Based on these results, we made a decision to incorporate more active learning in instructional presentations.

Several survey questions asked why and how frequently students use various library services and collections. Not surprisingly, the most frequent library activities were studying and talking with friends. Use of government documents was disappointing. Even though the workbook included government documents, 93 percent of the sophomores reported that they had "never" or "hardly ever" used such documents. This use pattern influenced the library to load government documents into the on-line catalogue, where students would find them along with books and other materials, instead of having to look in a separate index.

Learning to use the library is closely tied to course-related assignments. No matter how effective instruction is, students need to practice skills to strengthen and retain them. Student estimates of the portion of their courses that required use of the library, excluding reserves, are shown below.

Student Estimate of Portion of Courses Requiring Library Use, Excluding Reserves	Percentage*
Hardly any	24
About one-fourth	34
About one-half	24
About three-fourths	10
Nearly all	10

*Due to rounding, percentages add up to more than 100 percent.

Fifty-eight percent of the students reported that one-fourth or less of their courses required them to use the library. With the emphasis at JMU on writing, problem solving, and critical thinking, the percentage of courses making library assignments was lower than expected. Lower-division courses at JMU frequently have a larger number of students than upper-division courses, making it more difficult for professors to grade papers and other open-ended assignments. The results of this question had a strong impact on our instruction program. As liaison librarians, we began making it our business to work with faculty to develop good library assignments. When class size was large, we tried to develop creative assignments that would be easy to grade.

Throughout our assessment efforts, we have found that when one question is answered, it raises even more. This was one of those instances. We immediately wanted to compare these data from sophomores with data from seniors to see if courses in the majors had more library assignments. We also wanted to know how sophomores would compare with freshmen on the test. The answer would tell us whether our instruction program was having an impact.

Freshman and Sophomore Results Compared

That year, 1990, we expanded the length of the test to forty-six items and administered the longer test to entering freshmen on August Assessment Day. Freshmen scored surprisingly well on the test, showing a high baseline of knowledge. A year and a half later, we tested many of the same students, by then second-semester sophomores, using the same test. Students at the sophomore level performed much better than they had as freshmen. In fact, they scored a whole standard deviation higher, which is considered statistically significant. This suggests that our instruction program, in combination with course-related assignments and other experiences, was helping students gain needed skills.

When we revised the test, we identified a total of thirty-two items, some old and some new, that addressed the skills specified in the *Standards of Learning Objectives for Virginia Public Schools: Library/Information Use* (Virginia Department of Education, 1986). Surprisingly, freshmen performed very poorly on this subscore, even though three-fourths had graduated from Virginia high schools and 98 percent had received library instruction in elementary or secondary schools. Forty percent scored "incompetent," and another 27 percent scored "minimally competent." Apparently, Virginia high school graduates had not learned the objectives stated in the standards.

Additional Benefits of Assessment

When JMU came up for its decennial accreditation review by the Southern Association of Colleges and Schools (SACS) in 1990 and again in 2000, the library presented a full report of assessment results and received a very positive response from SACS. Other accrediting bodies have since begun to call for evidence that students have life-long learning skills. Over the years, JMU has received a great deal of affirmation from the Virginia State Council of Higher Education for assessment efforts in this area, as well as from visiting teams reviewing our programs in general education and in the majors.

This method of assessing information competence by administering a multiple-choice, pencil-and-paper test to a random sample of students had served us well for several years. Each year we would revise the test, administer it, and interpret the results. It was an economical way to assess library skills, and it provided a good way to evaluate the effectiveness of our program. It did, however, have some drawbacks:

- Not every student had to take the test.

- Students might not be motivated to do their best, since the scores did not count.

- The test was a good measure of knowledge but not of the ability to apply knowledge.

- The Library Skills Test focused on students' ability to use libraries. Technology was changing the information world, and skills in finding and evaluating information went beyond the walls of the library.

- Many of the test questions measured knowledge of specific sources and software, rather than concepts and transferable skills.

These factors, along with changes in our general education program, led us to the development of a new model of curriculum-integrated information literacy, with a required on-line competency test that all students would have to pass.

Competency-Based Program for Information Literacy

Common Objectives

In the mid-1990s, the JMU general education program was rebuilt from the ground up, using a competency-based model. Faculty developed common learning objectives that all general education students would be required to achieve. Every student in the program would have to demonstrate mastery of the skills. First-year students would take basic skills courses that met objectives in five areas: writing, communication, critical thinking, technology, and information literacy.

Information literacy was included in the new program because faculty recognized that knowledge and skills in finding and evaluating information are fundamental both for successful completion of coursework and for life after graduation. Library skills had, after all, been taught in English 101 and 102 for over a decade through use of the *Library Skills Workbook*. Also, the coordinator of library instruction, a member of the General Education Goals and Objectives Committee, was able to advocate learning objectives relating to information-seeking and information evaluation skills. Two of the eighteen learning objectives for the new program relate to information literacy:

- Formulate and conduct an information search that includes a variety of reference sources, such as encyclopedias, library catalogs, indexes, bibliographies, statistics sources, government publications, and resources available on the Internet.

- Evaluate information sources in terms of accuracy, authority, bias, and relevance in written and oral contexts (James Madison University General Education Office, 1995, pp. 8-9).

In addition, students are expected to learn word processing and presentation software, skills later defined as being important to information literacy in the *Information Literacy Competency Standards for Higher Education* (Association of College and Research Libraries, 2000).

Beginning with these two program objectives for information literacy, librarians and faculty developed a more specific list of behavioral learning objectives. This list became the basis for our entire information literacy program. New general education courses, assignments, our instruction program, and our assessment test worked together toward the same end—for all students to learn the stated objectives.

From Workbook to Web-Based Instruction

Two coinciding changes influenced our library to move from instruction using a workbook to Web-based instruction: the emergence of the Internet as the main way that information is stored and accessed, and the new competency-based general education program. Increasing use of the Internet had a dramatic impact on libraries, changing the way we functioned and the way that students found information. During this time of rapid change, it became harder and harder to keep a print workbook up to date. At the same time, we wanted to develop an instruction program that would address the new general education objectives for information literacy. In response to both changes, we developed Go for the Gold (James Madison University Libraries, 1996–2002), a Web-based program consisting of eight instructional modules.

The transition from a library workbook to a Web-based instruction program was somewhat bumpy. The workbook had exercises that required walking around the library. The earliest version of Go for the Gold had none; it was merely text and illustrations. The Web-based program was easier to update and more accessible to students anytime and anywhere, but it had some shortcomings. Faculty had no way of knowing whether students had read and studied the eight modules comprised in the program. We had no evidence that the program would be effective. As we moved to this new form of instruction, we hoped that assessment would answer several questions:

- How many students were actually using Go for the Gold?

- What did the students think of Go for the Gold as a learning tool?

- Were they learning important skills by reading and studying the eight learning modules?

- Were those who used Go for the Gold performing better on the test than those who did not use it?

- What improvements needed to be made in Go for the Gold?

New data from the Library Skills Test provided student ratings of the helpfulness of Go for the Gold:

	Percentage
Very helpful	9
Somewhat helpful	64
Not very helpful	21
Not helpful at all	5

The data told us that 73 percent of the students who had used Go for the Gold reported it to be "somewhat helpful" or "very helpful." These ratings were good, but not as good as the 81 percent who had rated the workbook as "useful" or "very useful."

We also collected data on how many students had completed the Go for the Gold modules:

Portion of Go for the Gold Completed	Percentage
Completed all eight modules	45
Completed some modules	27
Did not complete any modules	28

The survey ratings on the helpfulness of Go for the Gold were encouraging; however, we found that only 45 percent of the students had completed all eight modules. Twenty-eight percent had not used Go for the Gold at all. Since this was the only form of instruction for beginning students, this was a matter of great concern to English faculty and librarians alike.

Based on these assessment data, we were able to make improvements in Go for the Gold that served us well. With help from a library programmer, we added on-line exercises for each of the eight modules in 1997. Students answered a set of multiple-choice questions for each module. Some of the questions required them to apply knowledge by finding information in the catalogue and in databases. Students received immediate feedback on their performance and then were prompted to e-mail their score to faculty. Although these exercises engaged students actively, the method of reporting scores proved cumbersome to faculty as the volume of e-mail soared. In 1999, our library programmer developed a database that stored the scores. It interfaced with the campus authentication database to ensure that each student had a unique record. Faculty could log on and see all of their students' scores for all eight modules in one table. This was much better, as it eliminated e-mail and allowed faculty to see the scores at their convenience. Students could also view their own scores.

By storing the scores in a database, the library could count the number of students who had completed Go for the Gold exercises, and we could tell exactly how many and which modules they used. In 2001–2002, 3,333 first-year students used the program. Being able to count Go for the Gold users in this way complemented our assessment survey questions and was undoubtedly more reliable than student reports of module use.

Assessment results proved to be very useful in evaluating the effectiveness of Go for the Gold. Both student ratings and the number of users were interesting, but we wanted to know if completing the modules actually resulted in student learning. To answer this question, we looked at the data in two ways. First, we looked at students who had completed all of the modules, some of the modules, and none of the modules. We compared the mean scores of these three groups. There was no significant difference in scores, as shown in Table 7.3.

Another way that we tried to answer this question was to look at 496 students who took the ISST twice, on different days. At the time of the first test, the students had completed none or some of Go for the Gold. At the time of the second test, 443 reported no increase in Go for the Gold usage, and 53 students reported that they had completed additional exercises (that is, their responses had changed from none to some or all, or from some to all). We compared the test scores of these two groups. Both groups increased their scores by about the same amount, providing no meaningful evidence that completing Go for the Gold improved students' test scores.

The impact of a learning intervention is difficult to measure, and we do not want to draw too many conclusions. Previously, however, we had been able to record a significant gain in scores after students completed the *Library Skills Workbook*. Going back to a print workbook is not a viable option, but if we could find out why the workbook

Table 7.3. Mean Test Scores, by Portion of Go for the Gold Completed

Portion of Go for the Gold (GFTG) Completed	Number of Students	Mean Total Test Score
Completed all GFTG exercises	1,763	43.84
Completed some of the GFTG exercises	648	43.98
Did not complete any GFTG exercises	260	43.77

Table 7.4. ISST Score Improvement, by Change in Go for the Gold Completion

Portion of Go for the Gold Completed at Second Test Compared with First Test	Mean Score on First Test	Mean Score on Second Test	Improvement
Completed more of Go for the Gold (n = 53)	37.4	44.7	7.3
Did not complete more of Go for the Gold (n = 443)	38.2	44.2	6.0

was more effective, we might be able to improve Go for the Gold. The workbook required students to find answers by using their tactile, kinetic, aural, and visual senses to take in information. Our Web-based instruction at that time was completely visual and could be completed without setting foot in the library. Subsequently, we developed a one-page library tour exercise that general education faculty can use to supplement Go for the Gold, providing students with an experience in the library. Our plans include finding ways to make Go for the Gold a more effective tool, and assessment data may help us find out what we need to do.

The On-Line Information-Seeking Skills Test

Soon after Go for the Gold replaced the workbook, we developed a new test to address the weaknesses of the assessment program. This Information-Seeking Skills Test goes beyond the old Library Skills Test and measures concepts and transferable skills, with strong emphasis on evaluation of information, which has become more important than ever because of the uncontrolled nature of the Internet and students' growing reliance on it as a source of information. We avoided questions that measure knowledge of specific software or sources.

A second weakness of our old pencil-and-paper test was that it had never effectively measured the ability to find information. The new test employs a Web-based format with HTML frames that more effectively measures students' ability to apply knowledge by searching for information. Questions are displayed in the lower frame, and students search for answers in the upper frame, using the on-line catalogue, databases, and the Internet. With two frames, students can see a question and search for the answer at the same time. The test also includes multiple-choice knowledge questions, adapted from the earlier Library Skills Test. As shown in the blueprint below, the ISST is composed of fifty-three items, with four subscores that deal with the following content areas: reference sources, database searching, the Internet, and ethics. The test also deals with two cognitive levels: application and knowledge.

Subtest	Number of Items
Content Area	
Reference sources	19
Database searching	20
Internet	11
Ethics	3
Total	53
Cognitive Level	
Application	16
Knowledge	37
Total	53

The new on-line test offers many advantages, but a greater commitment of resources on the part of the library and the university is required to develop, administer, and maintain it. The on-line test requires the following resources:

- HTML coding of questions and answers

- CGI programming to score the test

- Development of a database in which to store the scores

- A server on which the test resides

- Computer labs, including both space and hardware, where the test can be administered

- Proctors for the computer labs

- Continual maintenance of links to the on-line catalogue and databases, which change frequently

Transition to a Competency Requirement

In the late 1990s, as we made incremental improvements to Go for the Gold and tried out the new Information-Seeking Skills Test, the general education program was evolving into a truly competency-based program. We learned that a competency-based program required a real cultural shift from the program we had had, which was based totally on course content and course grades. The new program is based on demonstration of competency related to a set of common objectives. As the program evolved, competency test requirements were instituted. Beginning in fall 1999, all JMU general education students were required to pass the Information Seeking-Skills Test by the end of their first year. The old test had been administered to a random sample; in contrast, every student in the program would be required to pass the new competency test. We could, therefore, make sure that all students had learned important skills before continuing at the university.

Setting Standards for Passing a High-Stakes Test

When ISST became a competency test, it was necessary to set a standard for passing, one that we could defend as fair. Led by assessment specialists, twelve general education faculty and librarians worked together in two half-day sessions to set a passing score. The group set two cutoff scores, one for "meets the standard" and one for "advanced." Using the Bookmark procedure (Lewis and others, 1998), participants were given the fifty-three test items, ordered by difficulty according to student performance on the ISST during the 1998–99 academic year. Based on individual judgments of participants, discussion, and then group consensus, the recommended cut score for "meets the standard" was forty-two items correct; for "advanced," it was forty-eight.

Students take the ISST, not on an assessment day, but any time during the year in a secure, one-hundred-computer testing lab, proctored by general education staff. Students show a picture identification and log on to the test using their JMU user ID. When a student passes the ISST, at either the "meets the standard" or the "Advanced" level, the accomplishment is noted on his or her transcript. Students may take the test multiple times, if necessary.

In 2002, the third year that the on-line Information-Seeking Skills Test had been required as a competency test, 85 percent (2,751) of first-year students had passed by the April deadline, a larger portion than in previous years. Still, 378 students had not attempted the test at all. Some had withdrawn from the university; some still had not heard about the requirement; and some had just plain procrastinated too long. (If students have not passed by October of their sophomore year, they are blocked from registering for second-semester courses.)

Student performance on the competency test is improving. Table 7.5 shows a gradual increase in the pass rate.

Dealing with Students Who Do Not Pass

Although 90 percent of the students pass after one or two tries, some students have difficulty even after taking the test multiple times. The library offers workshops and individual assistance for these students. We feared that demand would outstrip our resources, but it turned out to be small and manageable. Librarians who have

Table 7.5. Student Performance on Information Competency Test

Score	Percentage		
	1999–2000	2000–2001	2001–2002
Failing (0–41)	8	6	4
Passing (42–47)	70	66	67
Exceptional (48–53)	22	28	29

helped these students report that the main problems are test anxiety, inability to interpret bibliographic citations, difficulty with terminology, and general reading and comprehension problems. These encounters provided us with truly teachable moments. Students who failed were highly motivated to learn, knowing they had to pass the ISST to remain at the university. Nearly all passed after receiving personal assistance. Working individually and in small groups gave us an opportunity to listen to problems and find ways we could improve Go for the Gold as a learning tool.

To increase the validity of the ISST, we added several forms. With all first-year students taking only one form, answers can get out. Also, when students who fail retake the test, their performance improves because they learn the questions by seeing them again and again. Having several forms solves both of these problems. The new forms are randomly generated. A student who takes the test multiple times gets a new form each time until all have been used.

Faculty Workshops

Faculty education was essential to a successful transition to a competency-based program. With grant support from the general education office, the library offers faculty workshops every August, just before the academic year begins. Workshops focus on how to incorporate information literacy into general education courses. Faculty are encouraged to (1) assign Go for the Gold and make sure that students complete the modules; (2) make course-related assignments that reinforce information literacy skills and give students a chance to practice them; and (3) tell students about the Information-Seeking Skills Test requirement, the deadline, and the testing lab. The workshops were an effective way to inform faculty, but not all can attend. Librarians offer individual training for any faculty who are interested and send e-mail messages and other communications to keep all informed. Even with all this effort, it has taken several years to educate faculty and students about the competency requirement.

Assessment Versus Competency Test Performance

Librarians had long suspected that students did not do their best on assessment tests when the score did not count toward students' course or university requirements. By using the Information-Seeking Skills Test as an assessment test that did not count and then using it as a competency test that did count, it was possible to make comparisons. Students performed significantly better on the same test when it counted, as shown in Table 7.6. Improved motivation clearly makes the competency test a more accurate measure of student knowledge and ability.

Assessment of Majors

Assessing general education students has been the focal point of our assessment efforts at JMU, but liaison librarians have also collaborated with faculty to assess seniors in about fifteen majors. The academic program review process requires every major to assess how well it is meeting its educational goals. The guidelines for this review process mandate assessing "the level to which students are able to locate and use relevant materials" (James Madison University, 2002). This particular guideline provides an additional impetus to assess information literacy in the major, so liaison librarians are frequently asked to serve on program review committees. Completed assessments have in several instances revealed areas that need improvement, giving a liaison librarian and departmental faculty a rea-

Table 7.6. Comparison of Mean Scores for ISST as Assessment Test (1999) and Competency Test (2000)

	Mean Score on 1999 Assessment Test	Mean Score on 2000 Competency Test
Total test	77.4	85
General skills	71.5	80
Database searching	77	87
Internet	78	87
Ethics	90	93
Application	78.8	89
Knowledge	75	83

son for a productive conversation on the specific skills students need to know and how they can best learn them. Many departments decided to integrate information literacy into a required course as a result of assessment activities. In some cases, departments have integrated information literacy into their curriculum at the outset of discussions about assessment.

The assessment instruments for majors fall into two categories: paper-and-pencil multiple-choice tests and Web-based multiple-choice tests that use HTML frames. In each case, the librarian and faculty members begin by identifying learning objectives important to the discipline, developing a test blueprint, and then writing test items. The process is very similar to the one that was followed for general education assessment, which was described earlier in this chapter. Some of these tests have been revised year after year to accommodate changes in the curriculum and to make improvements such as updated course content. Some have been administered to a sample of students, and some to all students majoring in the subject, depending on the wishes of the department's assessment coordinator or assessment committee. Each of these assessments in the major is itself worthy of a chapter, but I am able to highlight only some of the findings that we found particularly interesting and useful.

- An assessment of senior English majors showed that half of the majors could not identify the *MLA International Bibliography* as the most important index for literary criticism. The same assessment showed that only one out of ten English majors knew the purpose of *Short Story Index*, *Granger's Index to Poetry*, and *Play Index*. The English Department responded by instituting a required capstone course with a research assignment. English faculty incorporate course-related instruction by their liaison librarian into this course.

- The Information Literacy Test for Psychology Majors includes a survey item about computer ownership. The data for five years show a dramatic and steady increase from 52 percent of seniors owning their own computer in 1998 to 96 percent in 2002. The same assessment of psychology majors showed an increase in the use of e-mail and the Internet over a five-year period but little or no increase in the use of databases or the on-line catalogue.

- A psychology assessment, like the Library Skills Test, asked students how useful they found several different methods of instruction. In 1998, three methods of instruction—*Library Workbook for Psychology* (Cameron, n.d.), instruction by a librarian, and individual assistance by a librarian—all received "useful" or "very useful"

Table 7.7. Frequency of Use of Computer Applications by Senior Psychology Majors

Computer Application	Percentage of Students Who Use the Application Once a Week or More				
	1998	1999	2000	2001	2002
E-mail	85	90	99	100	99
Internet	56	71	86	99	99
Databases, such as PsycINFO	10	8	5	9	9
LEO (catalogue)	9	7	7	8	10

ratings by 70 percent or more of the students completing the survey (see Table 7.8). Individual assistance received the most positive ratings. Beginning in 2000, students were asked about PsycTUTOR (Cameron, 2003), a Web-based instruction program with exercises that replaced the *Library Workbook for Psychology*. PsycTUTOR received higher ratings than the workbook. A librarian instructing the class in person received better ratings than either the workbook or PsycTUTOR. (These data are not consistent with general education students' preference for the workbook and Web-based program over course-related instruction by a librarian.) Preference for individual assistance by a librarian is consistent with general education student responses. We have found this preference to hold true across all majors we have surveyed. This finding, which is quite consistent over time, has important implications for maintaining reference and liaison services during difficult years when budgets are being cut and services reduced.

• In a 1999 assessment of psychology majors, 97 percent said that their professors made assignments that required them to use

Table 7.8. Senior Psychology Majors' Ratings of Usefulness of Instruction Methods

| Instructional Method | *Percentage* | | | | |
	Useful or Very Useful 1998	Useful or Very Useful 1999	Useful or Very Useful 2000	Useful or Very Useful 2001	Useful or Very Useful 2002
PsycTUTOR	–	–	55	63	78
Library Workbook for Psychology	71	58	49	55	n/a
Librarian instructing class	70	64	75	76	80
Librarian helping student	89	81	88	91	83

library skills in half or more of their courses, indicating a strongly research-oriented undergraduate program.

- Seventy-five percent of the geography majors made a competent score on the Information Literacy Test for Geography Majors (James Madison University, Center for Assessment and Research Studies, 1999). Their weakest area was database searching.

- Not surprisingly, seniors in the majors were often more confident in using the Internet than in using the library.

- Students in several majors, as well as general education students, consistently miss a question that asks the most efficient way to identify journal articles on a particular subject. Two-thirds of the students wrongly chose the on-line catalogue.

- About two-thirds of our students miss a question asking how to find out if the library has a given journal. They have performed poorly on this question at all levels and over a long period of assessment, irrespective of the library's moving from a print periodical list to on-line catalogue access and then to a separate database for periodicals. This performance has persisted despite a workbook, Web-based instruction, course-related instruction, assessment and competency tests, and reorganization of the library home page. One wonders if there is any hope for students to learn this!

Final Thoughts

At JMU, we learned a great deal from our early assessment efforts that helped us improve our instruction program. We are still learning. Assessment has been a wonderful impetus for important conversations with faculty about the importance of information literacy. Those efforts help us to work together to teach students these foundational skills. Having an information literacy competency requirement in general education ensures that students learn basic, critical skills by the end of their first year—skills that will be of real benefit in higher-level courses. Liaison librarians and teaching faculty who know that juniors and seniors already have basic information-seeking and information evaluation skills can target higher-level skills appropriate to the disciplines.

Although the development of an assessment program and a competency requirement has involved considerable resources at JMU, the payoff has been significant. The staff and faculty are engaged in a process of learning and improving what we do. Assessment has influenced decisions, from the choice of an on-line catalogue to the design of the library's home page. It has guided allocation of resources, causing us to bolster important services and keeping us from cutting services that are more useful than we had realized. It has even helped us decide what to emphasize in the classroom. Assessment is not an end in itself; it is a way to get answers to important questions that have to do with educating students effectively.

References

Association of College and Research Libraries. *Information Literacy Competency Standards for Higher Education*. Chicago: Association of College and Research Libraries, 2000. Also available at http://www.ala.org/Content/NavigationMenu/ACRL/Standards_and_Guidelines/Information_Literacy_Competency Standards_for_Higher_Education.html]]

Cameron, Lynn. *James Madison University Library Skills Workbook*. (7th ed.) Dubuque, Iowa: Kendall/Hunt, 1987.

Cameron, Lynn. *Library Workbook for Psychology*. Harrisonburg, Va.: James Madison University, n.d.

Cameron, Lynn. "PsycTUTOR." 2003. Harrisonburg, Va.: James Madison University. http://www.lib.jmu.edu/psychology/psyctutor/. Accessed Nov. 25, 2002.

James Madison University. *Academic Program Review Guidelines*. Harrisonburg, Va.: James Madison University, Aug. 23, 2002.

James Madison University, Center for Assessment and Research Studies. *Information Literacy Test for Geography Majors*. Harrisonburg, Va.: James Madison University, 1999.

James Madison University General Education Office. "Cluster 1: Skills for the 21st Century." *General Education Newsletter*, Oct. 18, 1995, 8-9 (the newsletter does not have a volume or issue number—just a date).

James Madison University Libraries. *Go for the Gold*. 1996–2002. http://www.lib.jmu.edu/library/gold/modules.htm. Accessed Nov. 25, 2002.

Lewis, D. M., Green, D. R., Mitzel, H. C., Baum, K., and Patz, R. J. "The Bookmark Standard Setting Procedure: Methodology and Recent Implementations." Paper presented at the annual meeting of the National Council for Measurement in Education, San Diego, Calif., Apr. 1998.

Virginia Department of Education. *Standards of Learning Objectives for Virginia Public Schools: Library/Information Use*. Richmond: Commonwealth of Virginia, 1986.

Conclusion: Continuing the Dialogue

Ilene F. Rockman

Study the past, if you would define the future.

Confucius

This chapter will provide a brief summary of key points and suggest strategies to continue the dialogue about integrating information literacy into the higher education curriculum as a university-wide responsibility. Such strategies include focusing on types of faculty assignments which can engage students more thoroughly in the principles of information literacy to better learn course content; the distinctive characteristics of the next generation of learners and their preferred learning environments; the relationship between information literacy and student outcomes; and efforts to accurately assess student information literacy proficiencies and skills. The challenge for universities in the coming years is to ensure that postsecondary students graduate with a mastery of information literacy skills and abilities. This challenge is growing especially acute, partly because of the following factors:

- The range of information choices continues to broaden.

- Technology continues to influence the behavior patterns of learners.

- Employer needs are becoming more complex and global.

- Trends toward distributed education affect the way in which instruction is delivered.

- Student populations are becoming more culturally and linguistically diverse, with uneven academic preparation.

- Institutions must repeatedly struggle to manage their resources wisely, given reduced sources of revenue.

- Curricular change is constant, needing to keep pace with present and future societal needs.

It is clear that we must transform the curriculum if we are to prepare students for a changing world (Jones, 2002) and give them the knowledge and skills they will need to meet real-life challenges in the years ahead.

The preceding chapters have focused on the themes of partnerships and faculty-librarian and intercampus collaborations; pedagogical and course content enhancements through the use of technology; infusion of information literacy into first-year experiences, general education, major courses, and interdisciplinary curricular offerings in both teaching and research institutions; embedding information literacy in teacher education, writing-across-the-curriculum, living-learning communities, distance education, and service learning programs; and assessment strategies.

All of these themes recognize that we have established a new learning environment for our students. Greater emphasis is placed on student-centered learning, collaborative work, critical thinking, data-driven decision making, analytical problem solving, and the ability of individuals to function as continual learners.

There is no doubt that information literacy is a critical teaching and learning issue for higher education. The uncertain quality and expanding quantity of many types of information (print, graphic, aural, spatial, and so on) poses new challenges for students. In addition, electronic information increasingly comes to us in unfiltered formats, raising questions about authenticity, validity, and reliability. Individuals who are knowledgeable about accessing, organizing, evaluating, integrating, communicating, managing, and understanding the ethical use of information are likely to be more successful at maximizing learning in college and after they leave the higher education environment, solving problems, and providing solutions in the workplace and in society-at-large. These individuals are the self-directed learners who are held in high esteem by peers and employers.

It is important to see information literacy in the higher education curriculum as a continuum of progressively increasing skills and knowledge levels that will lead to continual learning. As noted by Halpern and Hakel (2003, p. 38), "the purpose of formal education is transfer. We need to always remember that we are teaching toward some time in the future when we will not be present."

Information literacy has the potential to improve the quality of student learning and to equip students to be continual learners after they graduate. For this reason it has also been termed a "survival skill in the information age" (Presidential Committee on Information Literacy, 1989). It is especially important to integrate information literacy vertically (within the major) and horizontally (across the campus through programs such as general education) into the higher education curriculum because students are entering colleges and universities lacking this basic skill. Faculty want to see an improvement in the quality of student work, an increase in the effectiveness of student research, students taking more responsibility for their own learning, and students eager to engage in content to continue learning. Students want to complete assignments with less difficulty and more satisfaction and apply this knowledge to any new situation. Employers want to hire graduates who can take responsibility, solve problems, absorb and synthesize key concepts, organize and present information, and produce new ideas for the future. And colleges and universities want to graduate students who will reflect positively on their institutions and become learners for the rest of their lives.

According to the Wingspread Group on Higher Education (1993), "the nation's colleges and universities must for the foreseeable future focus overwhelmingly on what their students learn and achieve" (p. 13). This shift in thinking from a production mode of learning to an outcomes-based approach "includes not only what students know, but also the skills they develop, what they are able to do, and the attitudes of mind that characterize the way they will approach their work over a lifetime of change" (Smith, 2001, p. 29). Lindauer (1998) has remarked that academic libraries have an important role to play in influencing learning outcomes because they are key players in providing and structuring instructional resources and services to the campus community. She writes that "teaching library and information literacy skills is viewed as directly affecting student outcomes because these skills support such general/liberal education outcomes as critical thinking, computer literacy, problem solving, and lifelong learning" (p. 549). New regional accreditation guidelines underscore this sentiment with their strong support for integrating information literacy throughout the higher education curriculum and their recognition that information literacy helps to develop research and communication skills (Middle States Commission on Higher Education, 2003a).

Partnerships for Learning

Partnerships between librarians (who hold faculty or academic rank on several campuses) and discipline faculty are an excellent way to build information literacy into the curriculum. Partnerships can occur in institutions of any size and are helpful in supporting both formal and informal learning on the campus. There are several models for such partnerships, and each institution must find the right fit. Although faculty have traditionally viewed themselves as having sole responsibility for teaching, research, and the curriculum, this view is slowly changing. More opportunities for partnerships and collaborative efforts with librarians are becoming available, especially in teaching institutions, which recognize that faculty members have expertise in their subject discipline and that librarians have expertise that is conceptual, process-oriented, and interdisciplinary. Successful faculty-librarian partnerships are often focused on research strategies, the expanding pedagogical use of information resources, and the importance of developing creative, open-ended assignments as a means for teaching (and embedding) information literacy skills in the curriculum.

Course-related assignments can help students gain important information literacy skills, and faculty can benefit from the experience of academic librarians in this area. Assignments that are imaginative and focused on identifying, locating, accessing, evaluating, and integrating information into course content can lead to enhanced student learning by challenging students to think critically while engaging them in their own learning. These assignments can result in traditional written reports or less common creative expressions such as poster sessions, PowerPoint presentations, and Web pages, all of which can demonstrate students' mastery of information literacy principles through the application of knowledge to a new setting.

Examples of collaborative assignments in various disciplines have been mounted on the World Wide Web. These include the "Success Stories" posted on a Web site created by California State University, San Bernardino (http://www.lib.csusb.edu/infolit/SuccessStories.html), the "Biology Information Competence Assignments" on a Web site developed by San Jose State University (http://www.sjsu.edu/~cbhope/biology/infocomp/default.htm), assignments created by the Department of Black Studies at California State University, Long Beach (http://www.calstate.edu/LS/Black_studies.doc), and assignments in more than fifteen disciplines on the Web site of California State

University, Fullerton (http://www.library.fullerton.edu/information_comp/department.htm).

In addition, the University of Maryland University College has created a useful Web site to assist faculty members in developing information literacy and writing assignments (http://www.umuc.edu/library/infolit/intro.html). Included on the site is a tutorial for developing and evaluating assignments that promote effective research and writing in the disciplines; the tutorial also provides helpful suggestions for designing effective assignments that incorporate information literacy principles.

At another research institution, the University of Arizona, librarians and faculty work together both on creating assignments and in teaching technology partnerships that creatively integrate information literacy skills into courses as diverse as materials sciences engineering and theater arts (University of Arizona Library, n.d.). The library's Web page specifically notes that course descriptions and class assignments are a collaborative effort between faculty and librarians.

Experience-based assignments can contribute to deep learning (behavioral change) and transference of student knowledge from course to course. Such learning activities can also support inquiry, problem solving, and linking communication skills to coursework in a holistic fashion, all of which are advocated in the Carnegie Foundation's report *Reinventing Undergraduate Education: A Blueprint for America's Research Universities* as essential elements for preparing undergraduates for success in further studies or work (Boyer Commission on Educating Undergraduates in the Research University, 1998).

The Association of College and Research Libraries provides additional guidance for librarians on how to provide faculty members with useful suggestions for encouraging engagement and inquiry in research papers. The Web site "Characteristics of Programs of Information Literacy That Illustrate Best Practices" is targeted at undergraduate students, faculty, and staff at two-year and four-year

institutions (http://www.ala.org/Content/NavigationMenu/ACRL/
Standards_and_Guidelines/Characteristics_of_Programs_of_
Information_Literacy_that_Illustrate_Best_Practices.htm). Among
the best practices mentioned are librarians and discipline faculty
members collaborating and sharing responsibility for activities that
are centered on student learning. These activities may occur in general education programs, freshman seminars and first-year experience
programs, major programs, professional programs for teachers and
others, writing across the curriculum programs, service learning programs, distance education programs, or elsewhere in the curriculum.
What is most important is to provide challenging assignments and
multiple opportunities for students to develop important career and
individual lifelong learning skills.

Next-Generation Learners and the Use of Technology

To effectively teach in the contemporary higher education environment, it is important to understand the students we are teaching
(Oblinger, 2003). Traditional undergraduate freshmen were born
during the computer age and grew up in a technological world.
Although these students may have taught themselves how to surf
the Internet, download music, or send e-mail, they have not taught
themselves to be efficient in their searches, to evaluate the sources
of the information they are downloading, or to synthesize the information in a meaningful way. These students are computer literate,
but numerous studies have shown that they are not information literate (Caravello, Herschman, and Mitchell, 2001; Dunn, 2002).
Unlike previous generations, they are comfortable with multitasking
(completing coursework while listening to music, sending instant
messages, or chatting on a cell phone) and learning activities that
resemble playing a Nintendo game (that is, they are interactive and
experiential, and learning occurs through trial and error, rather than
in a linear fashion).

It is important to keep these points in mind when considering the use of electronic teaching tools such as on-line tutorials. Foreman (2003, p. 14) describes various aspects of the next-generation learning environment, one that is able to handle multimedia and complex technology and is ripe for innovative, interactive tutorials. He notes that the ideal learning environment is personalized and customized to the specific needs of the individual, appeals to multiple senses, and is constructive in that students can explore multisensorial learning environments that encourage the active discovery of new knowledge. An ideal learning environment also provides immediate feedback, motivates students to persist by engaging them in the content through the creative use of technology, and helps to ensure that concepts are committed to long-term memory for future application through real-world experiences. Foreman also notes that performance-based learning requires time and opportunities for discovery, analysis, interpretation, and problem solving.

These observations are consistent with the recent 21st Century Information Literacy summit sponsored by the AOL Time Warner Foundation and the Bertelsmann Foundation (http://www.21st centuryliteracy.org/). At the summit, new educational learning environments were discussed by the three hundred invited representatives from thirty-three countries. These learning environments included the ability of digital technologies to

- Foster access to information without the conventional limits of time or location

- Support customizable content based on a student's interests, needs, and capabilities

- Help students to actively redirect and redesign their learning experiences using multimedia applications

- Promote technological literacy (the ability to use new media, such as the Internet, to access and communicate information effectively), global literacy (the ability to collaborate effectively across cultures), and literacy with responsibility (the competence to consider the social consequences of media from the standpoint of safety, privacy, and other issues such as the ethical production and distribution of content)

Making the best use of digital technologies requires an accurate understanding of the habits of current students and their preferred learning styles in order to effectively design and develop technological programs that will expand and enhance their learning of information literacy principles, whether in teaching or research institutions.

Impact Studies

Information literacy instruction has had a positive impact in the K–12 setting, as well as in community colleges and universities.

Recent studies show that information literacy has a positive impact on student performance and student academic success (Glendale Community College, n.d. *a.*, n.d. *b.*). At the University of Texas at Austin, the use of instructional tutorials to teach a progression of information literacy skills through problem-based interactions in freshman-oriented programs, composition courses, business courses, and distance education courses has been shown to have a positive impact on learning (Fowler and Dupuis, 2000, pp. 343, 346). Project Better in the state of Maryland shows that integrating information literacy into content areas can lead to improved test scores, improved recall, increased concentration, and improved reflective thinking (Project Better, n.d.). Moreover, the work of Lance and Loertscher (2003), which summarizes and synthesizes research studies from more than 3,300 schools in eight states, shows that information-literate students result from information- and technology-rich environments in which teachers and librarians work together.

All of these studies point out the importance of assessing students to determine their levels of information literacy, to ascertain which models of information competency instruction are effective, and to evaluate the relationship between the library's information competency instruction and student learning outcomes.

Assessment Efforts and Strategies

The purpose of assessment is to engage a campus community collectively in a systematic and continuing process to create shared learning goals and to enhance learning (Middle States Commission on Higher Education, 2003b, p. 5). Students will learn more if instruction and assessment are integrally related (*Knowing What Students Know*, 2001).

Wright (1997, p. 574) notes the increasing acceptance of local approaches to assessment as opposed to system-wide, centralized approaches. This has been the case at James Madison University and several Northern California community colleges, which have tried to assess information literacy skills and abilities among their students. The development of specific valid and reliable instruments to measure students' information literacy skills has not been an easy task. Several institutions have made attempts, but only recently has the Educational Testing Service begun to discuss the importance of creating new diagnostic assessment tools to focus on information and communication technology (ICT) literacy at the higher education level (*Digital Transformation*, 2002, p. 10–11; *Succeeding in the 21st Century*, 2003). Such tools have the potential to help inform faculty, students, policymakers, and governing bodies about needed changes in the curriculum, new communication technologies, or instructional strategies to help ensure that college and university students can function successfully while in school and once they enter the ever-changing, technologically based workforce.

Colleges and universities have found that outcomes-based assessment (how a student may demonstrate information literacy principles at the beginning of an academic career) and capstone experiences (in which students demonstrate that they can integrate and apply their knowledge in the senior year with learning sustained and transferred from setting to setting) are both good assessment measures. Each helps both the student and the faculty member to see the degree of learning and the integration of that learning which is taking place. Entwistle (2001) notes, "students learn by understanding ideas and actively transforming them based on previous knowledge and experience, examining logic and arguments cautiously and critically, and becoming actively interested in course content." Competency-based information literacy programs within the general education program or major courses of study can help to establish benchmarks for this type of active student learning.

Unfortunately, many institutions choose to assess information literacy skills using only pretests and posttests. Although these instruments are easy to score, they do not fully demonstrate students' skills and abilities, since they do not capture actual student performances. Often, these tests are objective in nature (true-false, multiple-choice, short-answer, matching), paper-based, and administered at the beginning and end of an academic class to indicate change over time. They are not necessarily linked to performance objectives and do not demonstrate how well a student has learned to think critically and navigate through a search strategy process to find, evaluate, use, and apply information to meet a specific need. In addition, they are not often scenario-based, Web-based, or open-ended in their design and thus are limited in their ability to accurately measure student achievement. As Maki notes, "tests may measure how well students have learned information, but they do not demonstrate how well students can solve problems using that information" (2002, p. 10).

In contrast, when on-line tutorials contain behavioral, performance-based quizzes or tests for self-testing after each module, students (especially those in first-year courses) have a better chance to learn and retain new material. This form of assessment provides a unique opportunity for students to check their understanding of the information and to learn fundamental concepts that can be transferred from course to course, and thus contribute to their future academic success.

Embedded assessment—examining student work within a course—is another technique that can be useful for improving or advancing information competence skills and abilities (Rockman, 2002, p. 192). Embedded assignments, such as research projects or questions related to program learning objectives, offer students opportunities to demonstrate how well they have achieved course learning objectives.

Conclusion

The concepts and themes in this chapter reflect those included throughout this book. Transforming the higher education curriculum by integrating information literacy principles into lower-division and upper-division courses across the curriculum is a major goal of this publication. Such transformation will help higher education institutions to successfully prepare students for a changing world and the many challenges that they will face in the years ahead.

Information literacy—the ability to recognize when information is needed and efficiently and effectively act on that need—is *the* critical campuswide issue for the twenty-first century. Students must be given ample opportunities to develop information literacy skills and abilities in order to prepare themselves for a globally connected, technologically rich, and continuously changing learning society.

References

Boyer Commission on Educating Undergraduates in the Research University. *Reinventing Undergraduate Education: A Blueprint for America's Research Universities*. Stony Brook: State University of New York, 1998.

Caravello, Patti Schifter, Judith Herschman, and Eleanor Mitchell. "Assessing the Information Literacy of Undergraduates: Reports from the UCLA Library's Information Competencies Survey Project." In Hugh A. Thompson (ed.), *Crossing the Digital Divide: Proceedings of the Tenth*

National Conference of the Association of College and Research Libraries.
Chicago: American Library Association, 2001. pp. 193–202.

Digital Transformation: A Framework for ICT Literacy. A Report of the International ICT Literacy Panel. Princeton, N.J.: Educational Testing Service, 2002. Also available at http://www.ets.org/research/ictliteracy/ictreport.pdf.

Dunn, Kathleen. "Assessing Information Literacy Skills in the California State University: A Progress Report." *Journal of Academic Librarianship,* 2002, 28(1–2), 26–35.

Entwistle, Noel. "Promoting Deep Learning Through Teaching and Assessment." In Linda Suskie (ed.), *Assessment to Promote Deep Learning.* Washington, D.C.: American Association for Higher Education, 2001. pp. 9–19.

Foreman, Joel. "Next-Generation Educational Technology Versus the Lecture." *Educause,* July–Aug. 2003, 38(4), 12–22.

Fowler, Clara S., and Elizabeth A. Dupuis. "What Have We Done? TILT's Impact on Our Instruction Program." *Reference Services Review,* 2000, 28(4), 343–348.

Glendale Community College. "Information Competency Improves Grades." n.d. *a.* http://www.glendale.edu/library/icimproves.htm.

Glendale Community College. GCC Research Project on Information Competency. Status Report, April 2003. n.d. *b.* http://www.glendale.edu/library/libins/statusic.html.

Halpern, Diane F., and Hakel, Milton D. "Applying the Science of Learning to the University and Beyond." *Change,* July/Aug. 2003, 35(4), 36–41.

Jones, Elizabeth A. *Transforming the Curriculum: Preparing Students for a Changing World.* ASHE-ERIC Higher Education Report, vol. 29, no. 3. San Francisco: Jossey-Bass, 2002.

Knowing What Students Know: The Science and Design of Educational Assessment. Washington, D.C.: National Academy Press, 2001.

Lance, Keith, and David Loertscher. *Powering Achievement: School Library Media Programs Make a Difference—The Evidence.* (2nd ed.) San Jose: Hi Willow Research and Publishing, 2003.

Lindauer, Bonnie Gratch. "Defining and Measuring the Library's Impact on Campuswide Outcomes." *College and Research Libraries,* Nov. 1998, 59(6), 546–563.

Maki, Peggy L. "Developing an Assessment Plan to Learn About Student Learning." *Journal of Academic Librarianship,* Jan.-Mar. 2002, 28(1–2), 8–13.

Middle States Commission on Higher Education. *Developing Research and Communication Skills: Guidelines for Information Literacy in the Curriculum.* Philadelphia: Middle States Commission on Higher Education, 2003a.

Middle States Commission on Higher Education. *Student Learning Assessment: Options and Resources.* Philadelphia: Middle States Commission on Higher Education, 2003b.

Oblinger, Diana. "Boomers, Gen-Xers, Millenials: Understanding the 'New Students.'" *Educause,* July/Aug. 2003, 38(4), 37–47.

Presidential Committee on Information Literacy. *Final Report.* Chicago: American Library Association, 1989. Also available at http://www.ala.org/Content/NavigationMenu/ACRL/Publications/White_Papers_and_Reports/Presidential_Committee_on_Information_Literacy.htm.

Project Better. Maryland State Department of Education. n.d. http://www.mdk12.org/practices/good_instruction/projectbetter/information_literacy/general.html.

Rockman, Ilene F. "Strengthening Connections Between Information Literacy, General Education, and Assessment Efforts." *Library Trends,* Fall 2002, 51(2), 185–198.

Smith, Kenneth R. "New Roles and Responsibilities for the University Library: Advancing Student Learning Through Outcomes Assessment." *Journal of Library Administration,* 2001, 35(4), 29–36.

Succeeding in the 21st Century: What Higher Education Must Do to Address the Gap in Information and Communication Technology Proficiencies. Princeton, N.J.: Educational Testing Service, 2003. Also available at http://www.ets.org/ictliteracy/ICTwhitepaperfinal.pdf.

University of Arizona Library. "Librarian-Faculty Teaching Technology Partnerships." n.d. http://www.library.arizona.edu/partnerships/welcome.html.

Wingspread Group on Higher Education. *An American Imperative: Higher Expectations and Higher Education.* Racine, Wisc.: Johnson Foundation, 1993. p. 13.

Wright, Barbara D. "Evaluating Learning in Individual Courses." In Jerry G. Gaff, James L. Ratcliff and Associates (*eds.*), *Handbook of the Undergraduate Curriculum.* San Francisco: Jossey-Bass, 1997.

Index